The Sierra Nevada Before History

Ancient Landscapes, Early Peoples

LOUISE A. JACKSON

2010
Mountain Press Publishing Company
Missoula, Montana

Cover art montage: Sierra Nevada Mountains, photo by W. C. Mendenhall, courtesy USGS Photographic Library; Yokuts gatherers, steatite beads, and Yokuts basket, courtesy Bear State Books; desert bighorn sheep, courtesy Richard Rodvold, istockphotos

Printed in the United States of America

Library of Congress Cataloging in Publication Data
Jackson, Louise A.
  The Sierra Nevada before history : ancient landscapes, early peoples / Louise A. Jackson.
       p. cm.
  Includes bibliographical references and index.
  ISBN 978-0-87842-567-9 (pbk. : alk. paper)
1. Natural history—Sierra Nevada (Calif. and Nev.) 2. Sierra Nevada (Calif. and Nev.)—History. 3. Landscapes—Sierra Nevada (Calif. and Nev.) 4. Indians of North America—Sierra Nevada (Calif. and Nev.)—History. 5. Prehistoric peoples—Sierra Nevada (Calif. and Nev.)—History. I. Title.
  QH104.5.S54J33 2010
  979.4'401—dc22
       2010011971

 **Mountain Press**
PUBLISHING COMPANY
P.O. Box 2399 · Missoula, MT 59806 · 406-728-1900
800-234-5308 · info@mtnpress.com
www.mountain-press.com

To those who came before us

Contents

Introduction

THE PREHISTORY OF CALIFORNIA'S HIGH SIERRA REGION is more dream than reality. It is a story continually being rewritten, a story of times and events still shrouded in mystery; of ancient and evolving earth forces; of adaptive mountain animals and plant life; of prehistoric people, their beliefs, myths, and ways of life; of the interdependence of those people with one another and the land.

This book focuses on the southern High Sierra region, from its birth to the historic era. It encompasses the area of the range's greatest uplift, from Tehachapi Pass on the south to Sonora Pass on the north, and includes the major drainages of the Kern, White, Tule, Kaweah, Kings, San Joaquin, Fresno, Chowchilla, Merced, Tuolumne, Stanislaus, and Owens rivers. The region also contains today's Yosemite, Sequoia, and Kings Canyon national parks.

Based on a growing file of facts and evidence, this account is nonetheless bent through the lens of our own cultural perspectives and our tentative understandings of the prehistoric traces we have found. The best we can do is speculate what the mountains and the life within them may have experienced through millennia of evolution.

Geography

In some ways, the High Sierra is a portrait of everything we might think mountains should be: blue, cloud-speckled skies above intense green forests; granite spires rising from colorful hillsides; snowy peaks overlooking lush,

1

grassy meadows; deep canyons below necklaces of alpine lakes. But it is also unlike any other landscape.

As part of the western American Cordillera, the modern Sierra Nevada belongs to an extended family of mountain ranges that run the western length of North, Central, and South America. Within its immediate family, however, it is an only child, an individual range without the siblings of a full mountain chain such as the Rocky Mountains. It holds a distinct identity of its own, a landform more than four hundred miles long and forty to eighty miles wide.

According to a Spanish map drawn in 1778, a river named the Buenaventura created a continent-opening pathway that flowed from the basin of the Great Salt Lake through the Sierra to the Pacific Ocean.[1] For years, early Euro-American explorers searched for it. But it wasn't there. The modern Sierra Nevada is the only major mountain range in the continental United States that is undivided by any river or valley.

A 1778 map of the fabled Buenaventura River made by Bernardo de Miera y Pacheco, "Map of New Mexico with the latest discoveries." The river appears in the upper third of the map. —Courtesy Wikimedia Commons

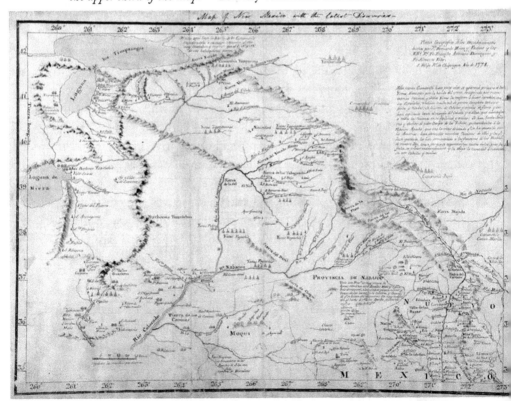

The Sierra's western edge lies far beyond its visible boundary, buried several thousand feet below the eroded sediments of California's great Central Valley. Overlaying its northern end are younger rocks of the volcanic Cascade Range. Still, its visual mass is so obviously one unified whole that, in 1871, surveyor Clarence King described it as "a definite ridge, broad and high, and having the form of a sea wave."[2] This wave rises from the Central Valley plains on its west side and breaks at the range's eastern crest to drop into the Great Basin deserts.

The Sierra not only rises from west to east, but it also rises steadily from north to south. Climbing from occasional 11,000-foot peaks north of the Stanislaus River, it culminates in an eastern crest where thirteen summits above 14,000 feet—including the Muir Crest and Mt. Whitney—form a 7,000-foot-long wall above the Owens Valley.

Then the range drops again. South of the Muir Crest, the peaks gradually become shorter, eventually rounding off into mid-elevation ridges. By the time the south-flowing Kern River's two main forks reach their confluence in modern Lake Isabella, most of the surrounding Sierra has become an expanse of gentle foothills.

The differences between the northern and southern parts of the range are striking. The northern portion's terrain slopes up gently from the west, flowing across heavily timbered ridges that extend to the desert on the east. It not only abounds with good lumber, but is also a recreationist's dream, blessed

Mt. Whitney, on the east crest of the Sierra Nevada —Courtesy Sequoia National Park archives

with easy access to low mountains, open valleys, forests, lakes, and waterways. The entire area is peppered with resorts, commercial centers, outfitters, and developed campgrounds.

In contrast, the southern Sierra is one of the most inaccessible areas of the nation. Today, only four fully paved roads cross its width, all between the Tehachapi and Sonora passes, and all but the lowest, Walker Pass, are closed in winter. From Tioga Pass south to Johnsondale lies a vast wilderness penetrated only by foot trails and stock trails.

There are few valleys between the Sierra's southern peaks, and most of these are uninhabited for more than half the year. On the range's western side, scattered small communities hug the foothills north of Kernville, with only a handful of summer resorts, power company facilities, and government centers bold enough to invade the highlands at altitudes up to 7,800 feet.

To the east lies the High Sierra, so designated by the Geological Survey of California in 1863. This region spans approximately 180 miles between Sonora Pass in the central Sierra and Cottonwood Pass in the south. More than five hundred peaks higher than 12,000 feet form a ninety-mile barrier along the eastern Muir Crest. West of the crest, the Great Western Divide and Kaweah Peaks create another barrier of 10,000- to 12,000-foot peaks, which separate the Kaweah, Kern, and Kings River watersheds.

"In the mountains of the Sierra Nevada . . . west of Mt. Whitney, and compressed within a small belt, can be found the grandest scenery in the world," boasted the *History of Tulare County, California*, in 1883.

> Here are to be seen three of the grandest ca–ons or valleys on the continent. . . . In these valleys are the highest water-falls . . . here are natural bridges and caves, extinct volcanoes to be explored, and living glaciers to be examined. The 'big trees' of this section surpass those of any other locality, not only in size but in numbers. . . . No part of the Sierras combines so great a variety of grand and instructive features as does this region with its towering peaks, its perennial snows, its ancient fossils and other exhaustless stores of study.[3]

Today, these wonders of the High Sierra region are preserved and protected in three national parks, two national monuments, three national forests, sixteen designated wilderness areas, and several state and county parks. In prehistoric times, the only stewards of the Sierra were the forces creating it—geologic events, weather patterns, plant growth, animal habitation, and a small number of human beings who dared to breach its depths.

The Great Western Divide, on the west crest of the Sierra Nevada —Courtesy Tom Burge, Sequoia National Park archives

The High Sierra of Kings Canyon —Courtesy Dan Hammond collection

Lyell Glacier. The forces of nature—volcanism, crustal movements, weathering, ice, water, plant and animal life—have shaped the Sierra Nevada. —Photo by F. E. Matthes (c. 1914), courtesy USGS Photographic Library

Forces of Nature

The modern Sierra Nevada, which began its rise from an ancient ancestral framework millions of years ago, is still growing. However, long before that, earth's internal forces created minerals, rocks, and crustal movements that led to the Sierra's birth. Deep convection currents of molten rock; moving plates of oceanic and continental crust; upwelling magmas; and atmospheric forces all have had their roles in creating the Sierra Nevada. The geologic focus of this book is on known events that have formed and continue to change the region.

The High Sierra provides life in abundance. The weather patterns it creates, the water it gathers, and the rich minerals of its soils all nurture life zones filled with hundreds of native plant and animal species. Their growth and adaptation to the earth's changing patterns have directed human habitation of the region. Only since historic times have the introduction of nonnative

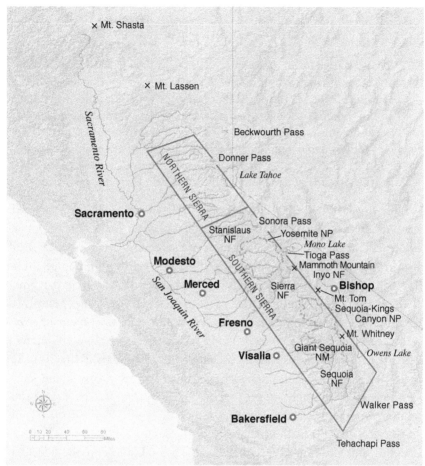

The modern Sierra Nevada —Adapted from USGS base map

plants and the loss of several animal species changed the patterns that sustained people for centuries.

Prehistoric Peoples

The early history of the region's human element is the most ephemeral to recount. It is based on limited and constantly changing archaeological and ethnographic studies as well as on historic myths and tales. None are definitive, none are complete, and all require interpretation. Most intriguing are the ancient stories handed down through generations, which are filled with tradition, myth, and magic. One such tale introduces each chapter of this book to help connect the reader to the early residents of the High Sierra.

In 1933 W. A. Chalfant, a collector of such stories, described the Indian storytelling tradition:

> The supernatural prevails in practically all Indian tradition. The native found it easy to ignore laws of nature when it became preferable to improve his tale. The storyteller had plenty of time, and when he had the center of the stage he made the privilege last. Consequently a great amount of detail was woven into each narration. . . . It was often told in detail, taking several evenings to end the story. Bearing this in mind, the reader may be willing to forgive the Anglo-Saxon directness [with] which some of the tales have [been] summarized.[4]

The lives of these early Sierrans held many similarities to ours as well as many differences—just as the cultural groups showed many similarities and differences among themselves. Chapters on the region's major prehistoric cultural groupings discuss the practices and beliefs held by all groups, but each also highlights a distinctive cultural element that was prominent in that group. The Tubatulabal, for example, were more matriarchal than other groups. The Yokuts were more socially organized than most, with distinct layers of governance and hierarchy. The Western Monache were renowned hunters and trade middlemen, while the Central Miwok were known for their ritualism. The Yosemite formed a distinct society by blending both the Miwok and Paiute traditions, often through intermarriage. And the Owens Valley Paiute placed great importance on shamanistic practices.

In all its elements, the prehistory of the Sierra Nevada holds both the universal and the unique. From the range's foundation to the advent of Euro-American infiltration, its prehistoric beginnings have led to all that we treasure today.

Petroglyphs and pictographs hold mysterious messages from the ancient peoples of the Sierra Nevada. —Courtesy Bureau of Land Management, Inyo archives

PART I

"When Lim'-ik, the Prairie Falcon, looked back over the mountains floating in the water, he saw that the range Ahl'-wut, the Crow, had built on the west of the great valley was much larger than the one he had built on the east." —The Great Western Divide, courtesy Laurel DiSilvestro

1. Geology

ORIGIN OF THE MOUNTAINS
A Western Mono and Tubatulabal Tale

First, Tro'-qhill, the white-necked Eagle, made the world. It was covered with water. Then, of mud from the bottom of the water, he made the land and all the old-time bird and animal people. For a long time, there were no mountains. They were made by Lim'-ik, the Prairie Falcon, and Ahl'-wut, the Crow. Lim'-ik was Tro'-qhill's son.

Tro'-qhill gave Lim'-ik and Ahl'-wut each the same amount of mud. Then he told them to build some mountains with the mud. They took the mud and flew away to the south. They began building the mountains at the place called Tee-hah'-cha-pee. They built to the north. Lim'-ik built mountains on the east side of a great water-filled valley, and Ahl'-wut built mountains on the west side of it. They worked for many years building the mountains. They could not see each other across the great waters, but they could see the mountains growing. Finally, they met at the north and made one big mountain together.[1] When they had finished, they sat down to rest.

When Lim'-ik, the Prairie Falcon, looked back over the mountains floating in the water, he saw that the range Ahl'-wut, the Crow,

13

had built on the west of the great valley was much larger than the one he had built on the east. Then Lim'-ik knew that Ahl'-wut had cheated him of some mud.

Lim'-ik told Ahl'-wut that he had stolen some mud, but Ahl'-wut only laughed loudly at him. Lim'-ik did not know what to do. He walked around and around and thought as hard as he could. Finally, Lim'-ik ate some Indian medicine. As he ate it, he grew very strong and wise. He flew over the two ranges of mountains and caught them, one in the claws of each foot.

Then Lim'-ik, the Prairie Falcon, flapped his wings hard and turned the two ranges of mountains around in the water until the large range that Ahl'-mut, the Crow, had made was on the east, and the small range, which he himself had made, was on the west.

That is why the low Coast Ranges are on the west side of California and the high, snow-covered Sierras are on the east.

—Adapted from Frank F. Latta, *California Indian Folklore,*
and Stephen Powers, *Tribes of California.*[2]

IF WE COULD LOOK FROM SPACE and watch the 4.5 billion years of earth's existence, we would see dynamic changes: a barren orb becoming covered with blue waters; the rising of continents above the oceans; surface movements creating new landforms; growing and retreating ice caps; the development of life in its various forms; the emergence and disintegration of mountains.[3]

But the changes go deeper, far into earth's interior, where forces of heat and compression create the changes we see on the surface. In its primeval beginnings as a planet, the earth's metals, minerals, and water compressed and heated to form a dense, molten-iron core at the center. Materials above the core separated into layers of molten rocks, called magma, to form the earth's mantle. Heated by the core, this malleable mantle began moving in convection currents, a process that continues today. These convection currents act like the currents in a pot of boiling water, with the hotter matter

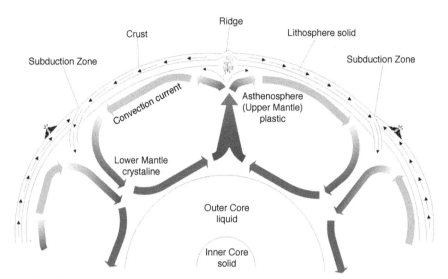

Earth's interior, showing convection currents that help create mountains
—Adapted from USGS, "This Dynamic Earth"

rising and the cooler matter sinking in a continuous circular flow. As flows of magma reached the top of the mantle, they entered the cooler asthenosphere, where the magma became solid enough to create a rigid layer of rock called the lithosphere.

As the lithosphere thickened, it began to crack, or rift, from the tensional forces roiling beneath it. The rifts widened, and magma and steam rose through them to earth's surface. Basaltic magma, which contains the least amount of the binding material called silica, was the most fluid and rose more easily through the rifts to the surface. The molten basalt spread out to cover earth's entire mantle and cooled into a three- to five-mile-thick layer of hardened crust. Granitic magma, which has far more silica content than the basalt and so is more viscous, rose in huge globs of gummy material. This thicker magma was often trapped below the basalt crust, but where it reached the surface it formed rising masses of granitic rock. These masses became earth's first continents.

As both basaltic and granitic magmas hardened into crust, gases and water vapor from volcanoes poured into the atmosphere. A dense cloud cover enclosed the entire planet until the crust had cooled and solidified enough that the water vapor could condense and fall as rain. For billions of years the rains fell, running off the granite highlands, weathering and eroding the continental masses, and flooding the basalt lowlands to become oceans.

Meanwhile, the mantle's convection currents continued to rise and fall. Their tensional forces broke the rigid lithosphere into twelve major pieces, or plates, with oceanic and continental crust riding on top of them. These plates covered earth's entire surface, much like interlocking pieces of a jigsaw puzzle, but they were not fixed in place. The convection currents beneath them kept them constantly moving over a flowing layer of elastic rock below their surface.

As they moved, the rifting continued. Rifts in the oceanic crust sometimes spawned volcanoes, such as those that form today's Hawaiian Islands. They also created long, underwater volcanic ridges in each ocean, some as tall as continental mountain ranges. From these ridges, basaltic magma from the asthenosphere flowed, spread, and solidified into new ocean floor. The ocean floor became part of the outward-moving oceanic plates on each side of the rift, widening the ocean surrounding the rift. Rifts in the continental crusts also caused widening, creating volcanic valleys that often filled with inland seas. Their landlocked subduction zones pushed up mountain ranges and sometimes pulled a large continent apart into smaller landmasses. This process of rifting, building, and breaking up is still happening today.

With the crust constantly gaining new material, it should grow thicker, but it doesn't, for what rises to the surface in one region eventually flows back down into the mantle in subduction zones. During the subduction process, the heavy, basaltic ocean plates on each side of the crust's rift dive under lighter, more buoyant continental plates through deep-sea trenches on the ocean floor. Some of the old oceanic crust is scraped onto the continent's edge to become part of the continent, but most of the oceanic material is carried down into the asthenosphere under the continent. During its descent, friction and heat from the asthenosphere melt portions of the oceanic crust, creating pockets of magmatic uprisings above which volcanic mountain chains are born.

As the plates move across earth's surface, they meet other plates moving outward from other convection rifts. When they meet, their boundaries undergo major transitions. Sometimes the meeting forms a subduction zone. At other times, the plates slide past each other, offsetting the boundaries of both. Sometimes several continental plates bind together to form supercontinents.

Some 800 to 700 million years ago, a change took place on one of these ancient supercontinents that would, millions of years later, lead to the formation of the Sierra Nevada region of California: the supercontinent known as

500 Million Years Ago
Rodinia began to break up around
800-700 million years ago; by 500
million years ago, proto-North America
was a separate continent

400 Million Years Ago
The continents were moving together

300 Million Years Ago
North America was colliding with
Europe and Africa to form Pangaea

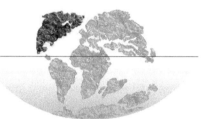

100 Million Years Ago
North America started moving
west and Pangaea broke up

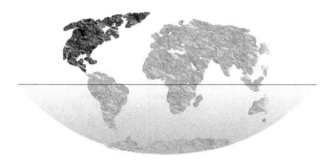

Today

Moving landforms —Illustration by Laile DiSilvestro, adapted from C. Scotese,
Paleomap Project, University of Texas

Rodinia began to break apart. Within 200 to 300 million years, it had dispersed into at least five smaller continents, one of which was the predecessor of North America.

Eventually, these separated continents began to move toward each other again, until North America collided with Europe and Africa to form a new supercontinent called Pangaea. Pangaea lasted only a few million years before it began to separate again, and ocean waters filled the rifts between the splitting landmasses. For more than 300 million years, a shallow sea covered the western margin of the North American continent across what is now California and Nevada. Coral reefs and sediments deposited along the shore and in the water were later metamorphosed by heat and pressure to form the oldest rocks in the Sierra Nevada.

About 200 million years ago, as Pangaea was breaking apart, the mid-Atlantic ridge formed along a rift separating Europe and Africa from the Americas, and the North American continent started moving west. As its leading edge met the Pacific plate boundary, the eastward-moving ocean plate descended into a subduction zone below the lighter, westward-moving continental plate. Rock melted into magma along the down-going ocean plate,

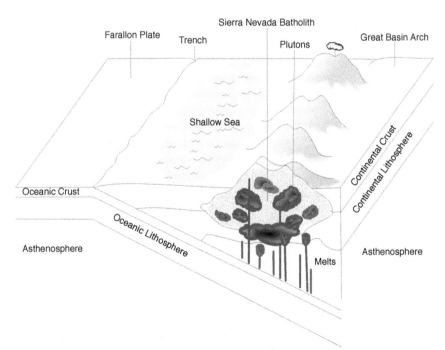

The Sierra's birth approximately 200 million years ago. As the oceanic plate subducted under the continental plate, hot magma rose through the ancestral range and eventually cooled to become the granitic batholith of the modern Sierra.

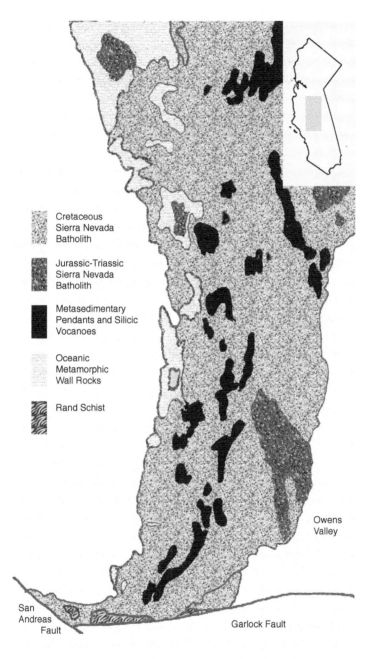

Cretaceous Sierra Nevada Batholith

Jurassic-Triassic Sierra Nevada Batholith

Metasedimentary Pendants and Silicic Vocanoes

Oceanic Metamorphic Wall Rocks

Rand Schist

Owens Valley

San Andreas Fault

Garlock Fault

Granitic plutons in the modern Sierra Nevada. These plutons in the Sierra batholith tell of the range's past. As segments of the ancestral range are pushed to the surface, a variety of rocks appear. —Adapted from J. B. Saleeby, Geological Society of America, Special Paper 438

and some of it rose to the surface as volcanoes. A volcanic mountain range formed along the continent's western margin above the subduction zone. This was the ancestral Sierra.

BETWEEN ABOUT 200 AND 30 MILLION YEARS AGO, the North American continent's western margin alternated between fault systems and magmatic uprisings above the subduction zone. During periods of fault activity, significant earthquakes were common. During the periods of rising magma, volcanoes erupted at the surface, but much of it also solidified in chambers miles below the surface to form intrusive masses of granite called plutons. Very large plutons, or assemblages of several related plutons in an area larger than forty square miles, are called batholiths. The Sierra Nevada batholith is one such body.

The Sierra batholith encompasses the entire mass of granitic rock that forms the range. The plutons gathered in it represent separate intrusions of granitic magma, each with varying compositions of minerals, textures, and forms. Surrounding the granitic plutons are sedimentary rocks—siltstone, shale, mudstone, and limestone—that were heated and pressed into new metamorphic rocks of slate, schist, phyllite, hornfels, and marble. Hot fluids that accompanied the magma circulated through the rocks, depositing minerals in cracks and fault zones.

The volcanic range that formed the ancestral Sierra Nevada was just one segment of a magmatic belt that extended from coastal Mexico through Idaho, northern Washington, and the coast mountains of British Columbia. It was once an imposing range, much like the modern Andes of South America. In what is now California, it ran northwest to southeast, in line with the subduction zone, and its streams flowed through valleys in the same alignment.

For more than 100 million years, the ancestral Sierra continued to develop above the subduction zone. During this period, the climate was generally wet and the range was lush with vegetation, and large reptiles roamed the valleys below its slopes. It was a short-lived range by geologic standards, for even while it grew, it also disintegrated as heavy moisture washed great rivers of sediment into a shallow sea along the western coast.

Those continental sediments mixed with debris from the pulverized coastline, rocks from ancient volcanic islands, and pieces of oceanic plate. These were pushed onto the edge of the continent to form corrugated wrinkles in the earth's crust, their folded strata forming gentle, rounded mountains separated by valleys and inland seas. With continuing deposits of new material, the continent thickened and extended westward until the Sierra's ancestral mountains lay far inland.

About 80 million years ago, the rate of subduction of the oceanic plate increased as a new subduction zone formed along the present margin of the North American plate, creating today's California Coast Ranges. Meanwhile, the ancestral Sierra continued to waste away until it only stood 3,000 feet above sea level. However, even as its surface was disintegrating, its granitic roots remained in place to become the core of the modern Sierra.

IN ITS FIRST EMERGENCE from the ancestral range 65 to 50 million years ago, the modern Sierra rose somewhat uniformly from a shallow western sea. But its second growth spurt was of a different nature. By about 30 million years ago, the Pacific plate was no longer subducting under the central California portion of the North American continental plate. The subduction continued in the Northwest and Mexico, where volcanoes remain active today,

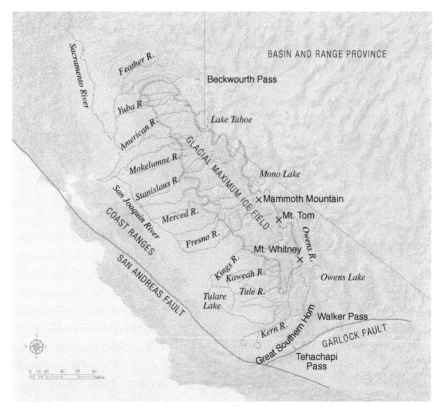

Geologic features that have helped create the modern Sierra Nevada —Adapted from P. Bateman and C. Wahrhaftig, *Geology of Northern California*

but in most of California the plate margin became a large fault system as the continent's western edge slid north. The San Andreas Fault, part of that system, continues to produce earthquakes today.

Faulting wasn't the only change; another distinct event was taking place. The entire Great Basin region, from the Rocky Mountains west to the Sierra Nevada, began to swell. From the Wasatch Range in Utah, through Nevada to eastern California, hot rock from earth's interior welled up beneath the region's surface. As the crust stretched and fractured, volcanic vents opened and spewed lava, coating valley floors with sheets of basalt. In the north, the basalt covered huge areas with mudflows that filled a growing gap between the Klamath and Sierra ranges and spread over their eastern plateaus. In the south, mountains rose and valleys dropped along north-south-trending faults. Huge blocks of broken rock rose, thrusted, slipped, and down-dropped in the cracking bulge of earth's crust—the Great Basin. The basin's swelling stretched westward until a shear zone (a narrow zone of multiple faults) between it and the Sierra Nevada began to form.

The pressures proved too much. Around 5 million years ago, with the Sierra batholith's plutons rising from below, the Great Basin's crustal swelling pushing against the growing mass on its east side, and an accumulation of eroding sediments increasingly weighing down the base on its west side, the faults along the Owens Valley shear zone split. The southern Sierra rose along major faults on its ancestral range's eastern side, causing it to tilt to the west.

In the past 10 million years, the eastern crest, including Mt. Whitney, has risen 6,000 to 8,000 feet. At the same time, the Owens Valley area has dropped, subsiding in one large block to become a valley between the growing Sierra escarpment and the desert Inyo Range. This process of uplift and subsidence continues today.

During this time, the growing range was also breaking away from the northern Klamath Range and working its way southward along its eastern shear zone. When it reached the Garlock Fault, at the base of southern California's Transverse Ranges, it curved westward into a bend now labeled the Great Southern Horn of the Sierra.

As the High Sierra region rose, it also eroded, relieving itself of most of its forbears' ancient materials. Streams that carried the sedimentary rocks down to inland seas and valleys followed the orientation of the ancestral rivers at their upper elevations, but in the lower reaches, they cut new, deeper channels toward the southwest as the tilting of the growing mountains continued.

High Sierra erosion patterns —Courtesy Tom Burge, Sequoia National Park archives

Even as it eroded, however, the Sierra Nevada retained some of the crust of its ancestors. Rocks that had crumpled long ago along the old northwest-to-southeast alignment now formed rows of sub-ranges above the granitic core. Almost the entire southern portion of the range contains segments of folded and twisted orange, yellow, and brown strata, remnants of ancient sedimentary rocks. Other ridges display dark volcanic slopes, the remains of ancient underwater volcanic uprisings.

On the west side of the High Sierra region, a secondary crest runs in the ancestral alignment along the Great Western Divide. Some of the metamorphosed sedimentary rocks, known as roof pendants, still exist at elevations over 12,000 feet in this thirty-mile-long divide and its surrounding peaks. Within these ancient formations lie caves. Over time, beginning as early as 200 million years ago, heat and pressure turned some of the limestone that had been deposited in shallow seas from the debris of coral reefs into marble. Eventually, water and carbonic acid dissolved portions of the marble roof pendants, forming caves. The High Sierra region has some of the highest-elevation cave systems in North America.

As if all the lifting and sinking weren't enough, the High Sierra also had to contend with a heavy load of ice. By 3 million years ago, the moving continents had enclosed the present northern polar regions, constricting circulation in the Arctic Ocean. In the cold climate, immense ice caps covered the northern third of North America. A cycle of ice ages followed, with fluctuations between warm and cold periods of approximately 100,000 years.

Although the North American continental ice sheets never reached California, that didn't mean the Sierra didn't bear its share of cold. Beginning as early as 3 to 1.8 million years ago, all the high mountains of the continent's western regions accumulated snow and developed glaciers. The northern Sierra was too low to be much affected, but the higher elevations of the central and southern Sierra collected spreading ice fields during multiple ice ages.

During a major glacial period, 60,000 to 20,000 years ago, a twenty- to forty-mile-wide ice field stretched more than one hundred miles along the Sierra crest, spawning glaciers as much as one thousand feet deep. On the western slopes, the glaciers cut their way down river valleys as far as fifteen miles, exposing the granite plutons of the Sierra Nevada batholith. It is this massive expanse of broken, sheared, jumbled granite that dominates the landscape of the modern Sierra Nevada.

High elevation cave in the limestone strata of an ancient roof pendant —Courtesy Laurel DiSilvestro

2. Climate

THE BIG WINTER
An Eastern Monache Tale

A long time ago, before my grandfather, his grandfather, and his grandfather, for many generations, a devastating winter came. Deep fell the snow for week upon week, until all the land of the Mono

"Deep fell the snow for week upon week until all the land of the Mono people, from the high mountains into the deserts, was covered." —Courtesy Wallace Woolfenden

people, from the high mountains into the deserts, was covered. So much snow covered the land that it did not melt until midsummer. The plants were buried deep beneath the snow, and all the animals died or went away to other lands. There was no place for the people to escape to, for the entire world was covered with snow.

The Mono people banded together at hot springs, where the warm waters might help them to survive. But they had no food. They held a council to decide what to do, and the aged people who were gathered there offered themselves. They sought their own deaths so the younger ones might be able to eat and live.

Only a few of the Mono people survived. It was a long, long time before there were many people on the land again, for those who had survived that winter went away.

—Adapted from W. A. Chalfant, *The Story of Inyo*.[1]

EVERYTHING IN PREHISTORIC TIMES depended on the climate. It was a constant force of change, determining weather, altering plant zones, modifying species, and relocating, creating, and destroying life. Between 4 and 2 billion years ago, scientists believe the earth's climate was warm and stormy, with the entire planet lying under a thick cloud cover. Slowly, low areas surrounding continental masses filled with rainwater caused by volcanic vapors. They became oceans, and algae began to bloom in the waters. As the continental plates moved across earth's surface, sometimes meeting to form a single interconnected land mass, emerging plant life could spread from one plate to another. When the plates broke apart, each one carried plant life into new climates, which often caused the plants to develop into new forms.

By the time the plates converged to form the supercontinent Rodinia, around 1 billion years ago, the warm rains had ended, and at various times ice-covered polar regions formed in different areas of the world. As Rodinia broke apart, between 800 million and 500 million years ago, a generally warm climate prevailed, and the first marine animal life developed between the drifting continents. For millions of years, rich soils and sands spread across North America's rifted continental margin and along inland seas, and flora flourished.

Then, around 250 million years ago, a catastrophic event occurred: earth experienced its first known mass extinction. It is theorized that the massive volcanic activity that took place over one-third of Siberia released huge amounts of carbon dioxide into the atmosphere and depleted oxygen in the oceans. This episode, sometimes called the Great Dying, destroyed 90 percent of ocean species and 70 percent of land species over a period of almost 10,000 years.

Several periods of massive volcanic activity have cooled the atmosphere to create changing weather patterns throughout the world. —Courtesy Sequoia National Park archives

When the volcanic eruptions subsided, plant and animal life began to recover, and new species developed. Among the new life forms that appeared were dinosaurs. By the time the modern Sierra began its uplift, 65 to 60 million years ago, the region was teeming with life. Then another event occurred that changed the climate for centuries. A large asteroid hit the earth, producing a cloud of dust and chemicals that filled the atmosphere, cooling the climate again. The event created another mass extinction, during which most of the giant reptiles died off.

Over the next 5 to 10 million years, a new climate evolved. About 55 million years ago, a hot spell began that lasted 50,000 to 100,000 years. The heat produced during that time, now known as the Paleocene-Eocene Thermal Maximum, created a temperature increase of 10 to 12 degrees Fahrenheit over most of the earth as it more than doubled the amount of carbon dioxide and methane in the atmosphere. The cause of this episode is unknown, but theories postulate that the rise in temperature may have been triggered by several forces that could have been occurring at the time. Vast volcanic eruptions known to have taken place under the North Atlantic Ocean may have disrupted the ocean's convection cycles that cool the water surfaces and surrounding landmasses. Earth's upper atmosphere may have lowered in pressure for long periods of time, creating changes in earth's jet streams and surface wind patterns, which in turn produced polar winds that pushed the sea ice out

The volcanic tablelands north of Bishop are remnants of volcanic eruptions and flows that changed the Sierra's landscape, weather, and growth patterns for thousands of years. —Courtesy Bureau of Land Management, Inyo

of the Arctic Circle, causing rising temperatures there. As temperatures rose, immense peat beds may have dried up and burned, filling the atmosphere with excess carbon dioxide, which created even higher temperatures.

Eventually, the climate changed again, becoming cooler and drier. The North American landmasses dried up, creating deserts and chaparral lands and depleting vast areas of sequoia forests. But along the crest of the rising Sierra and Great Basin areas, intense volcanic activity brought heavy rains, which changed plant growth patterns there, even destroying some of the flora in the northern Sierra with extensive mudflows.

A pattern of cool winters and warm summers continued to dry the land, and by 12 to 10 million years ago, deserts had started to dominate western America. Then, as the North American and Eurasian continents drifted to enclose the north polar regions, their climates changed radically. Between 3.1

A glacial landscape. Periods of cold created large ice fields and glaciers that covered the highlands of the southern Sierra Nevada at least four times. —Photo by G. Meier (1966), courtesy USGS Photographic Library

and 2.5 million years ago, the first known major ice age of the northern hemisphere covered large portions of the continents with ice sheets and glaciation. During this period, which lasted around 64,000 years, more forests died off, animals migrated to lower elevations or southward, and some of the destroyed plant ecosystems reemerged below the ice as wind, water, and animals carried seeds to a more favorable growth zone.

From that time on, the climate seesawed back and forth between glacial periods and warmer interglacial periods. A thaw some 536,000 to 476,000 years ago created huge freshwater lakes below the west and east sides of the Sierra. The next glacial period covered the northern third of North America in ice for almost 156,000 years. The Sierra Nevada lay mostly south of the ice fields, nurturing the plant and animal life that gathered there to escape the freeze. After the 90,000-year interglacial period that followed, the ice returned, but it, too, left little evidence in the Sierra at first. At the end of that glacial period, however, 20,000 to 15,000 years ago, heavy glaciation of the Mono Basin stripped much of the vegetation from the range's higher canyons.

Between 15,000 to 10,000 years ago, the continent's most recent interglacial period began. This warm spell brought drought, drying up the vast lake systems on the east and west sides of the Sierra. The plant and animal ecosystems moved to higher altitudes or northward. Then three short cooling trends occurred in succession: the first 10,000 years ago; the next 1,600 years ago; and finally, with eruptions creating the Inyo Craters on the Sierra's east side,

The Mono-Inyo Craters are remnants of volcanic eruptions 850 to 500 years ago. The eruptions created a cold weather pattern such as that described in the Eastern Monache tale "The Big Winter."
—Courtesy USGS Volcano Hazard Program, Long Valley

from 850 to 500 years ago. Each produced small cirque glaciers throughout the highlands. With each change in climate, flora and fauna changed with it, with some species dying out, others evolving, many moving, and some hanging on, clinging to life, then flourishing once again.

By the time humans began to settle in California, as early as 20,000 years ago, the High Sierra region held most of its modern configurations. Millions of years of major uplifts had defined the peaks and canyons. The last major glacial period had widened valleys and created mountain passes. The vegetation was settling into ecosystems defined by various zones of optimum growth. These ecosystems were and still are constantly affected by the variations of weather patterns, largely created by the High Sierra's own form.

THE HIGH ELEVATION OF THE SOUTHERN SIERRA creates weather patterns that affect each zone. The 12,000- to 14,000-foot peaks of the Great Western Divide and eastern Muir Crest serve as barriers to most of the storm systems passing through from the Pacific Ocean. They catch the moisture in the forested zones of the west side while creating a rain shield for the arid slopes above the eastern deserts.

The high ridge of the Kings-Kern Divide has a pronounced effect on storm patterns. Its short, west-to-east alignment of 12,000- to almost 14,000-foot peaks impedes the storms that sweep down from the Gulf of Alaska. North of the divide, the precipitation from a Pacific storm can be three to four times heavier than it is south of it.

The Kings-Kern Divide stops many of the winter storms that sweep down from the arctic regions, preventing them from reaching the Sierra's southernmost regions.
—Photo by F. E. Matthes (1925), courtesy USGS Photographic Library

Several conditions exist that should prevent the southern Sierra from ever seeing heavy precipitation. Besides the various crests and divides that block storms from the north, the Coast Ranges catches most of the moisture from warm western Pacific systems before they ever reach the Sierra. Only a northern opening at San Francisco Bay's Golden Gate allows the full force of Pacific storms to make it past the coastal mountains. During winter, high-pressure systems also hover over California's central valleys and often deflect storms northward. In spite of these obstacles, the High Sierra builds heavy snowpack most winters and generates large thunderstorms each summer. This is because the height of the mountains causes the region to create its own weather patterns.

Even after most of a storm's moisture has fallen on the coastal mountains, the residual storm clouds that drift over the central valleys bump against the mountains and get caught there. At the same time, the warm flow of air pushing inland from the Pacific is forced upward by the Sierra. As the air cools, approximately one degree Fahrenheit for each three hundred feet of rise in altitude, its capacity for holding water diminishes. So when the entire moist air mass is pushed up into the cooler mountain atmosphere, moisture condenses and falls once again.

Spring and summer thunderstorms generate much of the moisture that falls annually in the High Sierra region. —Courtesy Tom Burge, Sequoia National Park archives

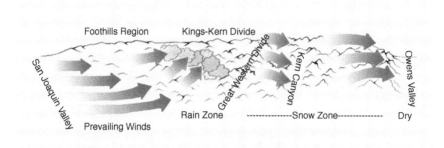

Southern Sierra weather patterns —Adapted from Sequoia National Park archives map

Prevailing winds from the Pacific tend to strike the western Sierra at an elevation of around 4,000 feet, banking the clouds above that level and creating a dry foothill region below. The greatest amounts of precipitation in the central and southern Sierra occur at the 5,000- to 9,000-foot levels, helping to create the wide coniferous forest zones of those elevations. The heaviest precipitation occurs in the upper yellow pine belt, where the *Sequoia dendron gigantea* (giant sequoias) grow. Above the 8,000- to 9,000-foot level, the amount of precipitation decreases quickly. As the winds rise up the mountain, the moisture is released until little is left at the top. In the highest regions, the peaks receive so little moisture that they often stand stark and rocky above the lower snowfields during major winter storms. Even during the ice ages, the glaciers could not build up enough ice to cover the highest alpine slopes.

On the eastern slopes of the High Sierra region, most of the rainfall occurs in summer. Historically, the eastern crest rising above the Owens Valley receives more moisture in August than in any other month. Fast-growing formations of cumulus clouds build over the peaks whenever moist air flows from the Pacific across the hot San Joaquin Valley, then rises to an elevation cold enough to create them. Their flat bottoms mark the line of condensation. After two to five days of buildup, they often develop into heavy thunderstorms that provide relief to the thirsty desert landscape.

Throughout the millennia, rain, snow, ice, heat, drought, running water, and wind have exposed and scoured the metamorphic and granite rocks of the High Sierra region. As they disintegrated, those rocks became mineral-rich soils in which an amazing variety of plants could grow.

3. Vegetation

THE CREATION OF LAND
An Owens Valley Paiute Tale

Long, long ago, many beings lived on the peak of Ow-wah-ne when this country was under water.[1] For a period of time, these beings pleaded with Nature for land and dived in the depths of the water to find soil. All kinds of waterfowl attempted to reach the bottom, except one who is known as the Helldiver, who took no interest in what was going on.

The coyote, who was distrusted and hated by most everyone, would plunge into the water and bring up a grain or two of sand and offer it as proof that he had dived to the bottom. But there was no doubt he had placed it under his fingernails before making the plunge.

After every other being had tried, they called on the Helldiver. He told them it was impossible to reach bottom, but he would try, so he plunged into the deep blue water and stayed under longer than anyone else who had tried. When he came up, he assured them it was no use to try, but others pleaded with him, so he dived again. This time he stayed longer, but when he at last popped up, he refused to dive any more, stating that there was danger of drowning.

34

"Long, long ago, many beings lived on the peak of Ow-wah-ne when this country was under water." Ow-wah-ne was the Paiute name for Mt. Tom, which lies south of Mammoth Mountain. All Sierra prehistoric peoples had tales of the creation of land out of water. —Courtesy Wallace Woolfenden

After several days of coaxing by his friends and others, the Helldiver promised to make one last dive at dawn the following day. When light began to break in the east, the beings gathered to witness the dive. As the morning star peeped over the horizon, the Helldiver stood facing in that direction over the silvery water, pleading with

Nature for strength and endurance. When the morning star ascended high into the sky, the Helldiver plunged easterly straight into the water and did not return.

It was near noon when the anxious crowd concluded that the Helldiver had drowned. The coyote cried and sang funeral songs, and the beings carried on a regular funeral ceremony. Suddenly, the Helldiver came to the top and made his way to shore. He offered a handful of fertile soil and distributed it over the great water a little at a time, as if sowing grain. Soon the water began to lower. Islands and valleys popped up as water pooled into lakes, rivers, and creeks. The mountains and the whole country seemed to turn green overnight as vegetation grew.

—Adapted from W. A. Chalfant, *The Story of Inyo*.[2]

AROUND 220 TO 150 MILLION YEARS AGO, North America, Asia, and Europe were covered with extensive forests. During the time of the ancestral Sierra Nevada, tropical broad-leafed and evergreen forests grew on its slopes. As the modern Sierra Nevada began to rise, a cooling period enlarged the coniferous forest and helped the giant sequoia proliferate. At the same time, however, the range's uplift also helped to create dry regions.

The Sierra Nevada has been described as an oasis surrounded by deserts. While the region has its share of dry spots, without the water that flows from the mountains, all of inland California would be arid, with limited plant growth. Instead, the Sierra's rivers and streams wash hundreds of feet of nutrient–rich soil down its sides, supporting its own plant ecosystems as well as those of the foothills and broad valleys below.

The plant life also helps support itself. In forested zones, the vegetation collects water and holds it for future use, while on land without heavy vegetation, rainwater and snowmelt run off quickly. During the ice ages, plant growth at higher elevations was limited by encompassing ice fields. The runoff from glacial melt flowed swiftly down steep, glacier-cut canyons to low valleys, where it formed marshes and immense lakes. During later, periodic wet

Coniferous forests of the High Sierra region —Courtesy James M. Cortez, Dreamstime

cycles, these lakes nearly covered the Owens, Sacramento, and San Joaquin Basins as shallow inland seas.

In late prehistoric times, the cycles of climate and weather patterns were critical to the High Sierra's first human occupants, for the amount of water determined where human habitation was best suited or even possible. In the past 20,000 years, as people first began to settle in California, a warming interglacial cycle created a wide range of climatic and ecological conditions with constantly shifting vegetation patterns.

When human beings first arrived in the Kings Canyon area, on the western slopes, a mixed conifer forest—which included western juniper and ponderosa, sugar, and piñon pines—existed in the low 3,000- to 4,000-foot elevations, where oak and chaparral lands now lie. The canyon also held incense cedars, California nutmeg trees, red firs, and some giant sequoia groves. Between 16,000 and 13,700 years ago, the Yosemite Valley was dominated by herbs and sagebrush. Then, as the climate cooled, these plants gave way to bunchgrass meadows and forests of lodgepole, sugar, and ponderosa pines; red and white firs; mountain hemlocks; incense cedars; and Sierra junipers.

Giant sequoia in the Tule River watershed —From author's collection

By the time the first people set up summer encampments in the southern Sierra, 10,500 to 9,500 years ago, the short period of optimal conditions for settlement was ending. Meadows at the 6,100- to 7,280-foot elevations began to fill with drier ecosystems. Firs invaded, and the forests lost much of their water-dependent understory growth, with mountain mahogany, manzanita, and sagebrush predominating.

FOR HUNDREDS OF YEARS, dry and wet periods alternated, defining what plant life grew. Eventually, though, an amazing process took hold. Starting 6,000 years ago, in what is known as a positive feedback cycle, increasingly organic soils promoted greater water-retaining capacities, which in turn created more wet-meadow ecosystems with even richer soils. Between the two droughts of AD 892 and 1350, a century of very wet soil conditions created many of the Sierra meadows and forests we see today.

The forests of the High Sierra changed often. During periods of prolonged interglacial drought, dry-climate growth crowded out new seedlings and filled up glades where water-loving shrubs and flowers could no longer grow. At the same time, Douglas and white firs and sequoias moved gradually up the mountains, while entire red fir forests receded as beetle infestations attacked them.

Two droughts occurred in the southern Sierra 900 and 650 years ago, lasting 140 and 200 years, respectively. During both, intense fires altered much of the area's growth patterns. While they killed some plant populations, they also provided essential nutrients, released the seeds of thousands of giant sequoias, and created open spaces where a new generation of growth could flourish.

TODAY, THE SOUTHERN SIERRA supports one of the most diverse plant ecosystems in the world. Everything about it—its alignment, its height, its geologic makeup—helps create distinct life zones. "After the sky has been washed by the winter rains, the lofty Sierra may be seen throughout nearly its whole extent," John Muir wrote of his first view of the Sierra Nevada, "stretching in simple grandeur along the edge of the plain like an immense wall . . . colored in four horizontal bands; the lowest rose-purple . . . the next higher dark purple, the next blue, and the highest pearl white—all delicately interblending with each other."[3]

High-elevation meadow at the headwaters of the Kern River —From author's collection

In prehistoric times, fires occurred frequently from lightning strikes. They were usually small, localized fires that cleared the underlying forest debris. —Courtesy Sequoia National Park archives

The rose-purple zone is the foothill region, "a waving stretch of comparatively low, rounded hills and ridges . . . the whole faintly shaded by a sparse growth of oaks and patches of scrubby ceanothus and Manzanita chaparral." In the dark purple and blue zones, giant pines, sequoias, and firs form "the noblest coniferous forests on the face of the globe. They are everywhere vocal with running water and drenched with delightful sunshine. Miles of tangled bushes are blooming beneath them, and lily gardens and meadows, and damp ferny glens in endless variety of color and richness." Above that, the white zone is "a vast wilderness of peaks, crests, and splintered spires . . . holding in their dark mysterious recesses all that is left of the grand system of glaciers that once covered the entire range."[4]

All mountains of the world are naturally divided into belts of vegetation, but seldom are the differences as pronounced as in the High Sierra region. On the eastern slopes of the range, because the gradient is so steep, the plant zones are compressed into tight bands and often intermixed. Rising from sagebrush-covered desert hills through piñon and Utah juniper forests, Jeffrey pines, mountain mahogany, aspens, and white firs gradually merge into moss-covered lodgepoles and red firs. Near the top, western white pines, hemlocks, Sierra junipers, white-barked pines, and foxtail pines begin to assert their dominance.

The surprise comes over the summit. On the western side, the alpine tundra of cushion plants and stunted conifers ends abruptly, dropping into a belt of firs, yellow pines, sugar pines, incense cedars, and sometimes sequoia groves. Not far below that, oak and gray pine foothills intersperse with broad bands of impenetrable chaparral, filled with chamise, yerba santa, fremontia, manzanita, and toyon. Below that lie grass savannas, with a scattering of oaks in the lower hills. Only in the canyons, where moisture, exposure, and temperatures vary, do the zones blend to any significant degree.

The elevation of these zones is not consistent along the length of the range. They vary according to latitude, exposure, temperature, moisture, drainage, and soil conditions. In the southern Sierra, the forests are open and grovelike, with large specimen trees of all varieties, while farther north the trees increase in density, creating a more compact and uniform growth.

Alpine tundra near Dusy Basin —Courtesy Tom Burge, Sequoia National Park archives

Depending on how tightly a given botanist categorizes the different regions, the Sierra Nevada contains from three to thirteen zones, defined by elevation, climatic variations, and plant communities. Each zone is sustained by a particular climate that encourages its own pattern of growth. Together, the zones create a plant population of more than 3,500 native species, hundreds of which grow only in the Sierra.

Each of these plant species had forerunners that adapted and flourished in varying climate conditions during prehistoric times. For thousands of years they have sustained an abundance of animal life, much of which remains today.

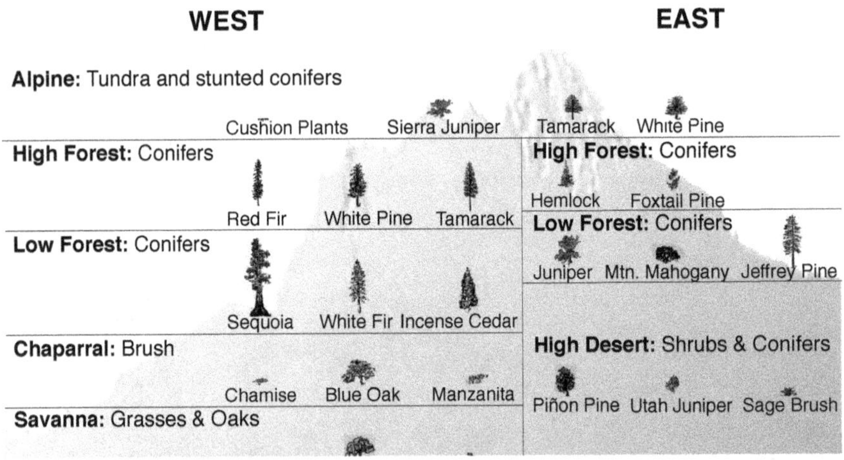

WEST   **EAST**

Alpine: Tundra and stunted conifers

Cushion Plants   Sierra Juniper   Tamarack   White Pine

High Forest: Conifers   **High Forest:** Conifers

Hemlock   Foxtail Pine

Red Fir   White Pine   Tamarack   **Low Forest:** Conifers

Low Forest: Conifers

Juniper   Mtn. Mahogany   Jeffrey Pine

Sequoia   White Fir   Incense Cedar

Chaparral: Brush   **High Desert:** Shrubs & Conifers

Chamise   Blue Oak   Manzanita   Piñon Pine   Utah Juniper   Sage Brush

Savanna: Grasses & Oaks

Sierra Nevada vegetation zones —Illustration by Laile DiSilvestro

West-side foothill chaparral —Courtesy Sequoia National Park archives

4. Animals

HOW THE ANIMAL WORLD WAS MADE
A Wukchumni Yokuts Tale

First this world was only the sky. A large tree grew in the sky. Only Tro'-khud, the Bald Eagle, and his son lived here. Tro'-khud became tired of flying around and lying in the sky alone. He said, "I am going to make the world." Then he made the world, all covered with water.[1]

Then Tro'-khud made Saw-wah'-kit, the Turtle. Next he made all the bird and animal people who can swim and dive in the water. Then Tro'-khud said, "We must have another kind of people." So he made Wee-hay'-sit, the Mountain Lion; Wee'-itch, the Condor; Lim'-ik, the Prairie Falcon; E-wa'-it, the Wolf; Ki'-yoo, the Coyote; Ow'-ih-chuh, the Fox; Tong'-ud, the Wildcat; Oo-pe-a'-e, the Dove, and No-ho'-o, the Black Bear. They lived together in the tree for a long time.

But Ki'-yoo, the Coyote, was mean and sneaky, and he spoiled everything. Tro'-khud saw that they could not live in the tree with Ki'-yoo, so he decided to make some land. He called all the water people to come to him. "I want all of you people to dive down into

44

"Tro'-khud became tired of flying around and lying in the sky alone. He said, 'I am going to make the world.'" —Courtesy James Brey, istockphotos

the water and get something I can use to make the rest of the world," he said.

All of the diving people tried hard to go to the bottom of the water and find something to make the rest of the world. But none of them could reach the bottom. Finally, Saw-wah'-kit, the Turtle, said, "I am going to the bottom this time and get something."

Turtle dived down and down until his front paws struck something soft. He caught a little mud in each paw and started back to the top with it. He almost drowned getting back, but Tro'-khud saw him come up and took him up in his claws so he would not drown. He opened Turtle's paws and took the mud he had found.

Tro'-khud and Wee-hay'-sit, the Mountain Lion, mixed the mud with seed of the shepherd's purse plant. They put the mixture in the ceremonial mortar and allowed it to stand for six days. The mixture swelled until it filled the mortar. All the water people crowded around under the tree. The people in the tree crowded around Tro'-khud.

E-wa'-it, the Wolf, said, "Let me spread it," so Mountain Lion let him do it. While No-ho'-o, the Bear, held the mortar, Wolf took some of the mixture in his hand. He asked Mountain Lion, "Which way shall I throw it?" Mountain Lion said, "First to the south, then to the west, the north, and the east."

Wolf did as he was told. By night of the seventh day, the water began to go away. At the end of six more days, it was all gone. Tro'-khud sent Dove out as messenger. He was gone all day. When he returned, everyone crowded close to hear what Dove had to say. "The water is gone," he said. "Only some lakes are left."

Then Tro'-khud said, "Everything is all right. We will go down to the new land." Then the tree came down to the land and became the Oak Tree, the first tree in the world. Then Tro'-khud made all the rest of the bird and animal people.

—Adapted from Frank F. Latta, *California Indian Folklore*.[2]

THE HISTORY OF ANIMAL LIFE in the High Sierra region is a long and complex story. It is told through evidence that scientists glean from soil samples, relicts, and modern technology.

Around 250 to 240 million years ago, enough of earth's marine and land animals managed to survive the first known mass extinctions to be able to continue their development.[3] By 220 to 150 million years ago, fish and shelled animals thrived in the seas, and reptiles, turtles, birds, and small mammals appeared on land. The ancestral Sierra was home to amphibians and large reptiles until 65 to 60 million years ago, when a catastrophic asteroid hit earth, the climate cooled and another mass extinction took place, during which most of the giant reptiles became extinct.[4]

As the planet recovered, land mammals took the dinosaurs' place—unitathores, elephants, creodonts, and the ancestors of horses, camels, and dogs. During the Paleocene-Eocene Thermal Maximum, high temperatures and drought caused mass extinctions of deep-sea species and created changing life forms on land. By 55 million years ago, mammals such as pigs, rhinoceroses, mastadons, llamas, saber-toothed cats, sloths, apes, and the ancestors of deer roamed the continents.

When the North American continent went into a major ice age, between 3.1 and 2.5 million years ago, the ice-locked northern seas lowered as much as four feet, and land bridges appeared. By 80,000 years ago, wooly rhinoceroses, mastadons, bison, elephants, horses, musk oxen, reindeer, and bears had crossed over the Bering land bridge from Asia to North America. About 11,000 years ago, as many as twenty species of grazing mammals lived in California, including horses, tapirs, llamas, camels, pronghorn antelopes, bison, mammoths, mastadons, shrub oxen, musk oxen, mule deer, elk, and bighorn sheep.

Museum replica of wooly mammoth —Courtesy Darryl Brooks, Dreamstime

The progression of animal species was not constant. Before 11,000 years ago, grazing animals were abundant in the Sierra Nevada region. But 10,000 years later, the Inyo Crater eruptions not only altered the eastern Sierra landforms, but also filled the atmosphere with particles that cooled the climate, changing plant zones and affecting animal populations. When a rapid warming trend followed, it created open forest ecosystems with shrub and sagebrush understories, which fueled intense fires. During these conditions, the mastadons, shrub oxen, musk oxen, horses, tapirs, llamas, camels, and bison all disappeared from the region.

Centuries before modern man arrived, the distribution of animal populations had settled into fairly consistent patterns. Although those patterns changed somewhat through the decades as drought periods and cold periods alternated, the animals of the High Sierra had an advantage over most species in North America, for the abrupt rise of the southern mountains gave them the ability to move relatively quickly to new locations during disasters and abrupt climate changes.

ALL ANIMALS REQUIRE A BALANCE IN FOOD supplies to survive. They need enough food to keep them healthy while leaving enough for new growth the following year. Each species population must remain large enough to replace those lost to carnivores, aging, and disease, but not so large that the food supply cannot regenerate. They have to find the right ecosystems at the right elevations with the right weather conditions. They must be able to find shelter in all seasons, and they must be able to survive varying conditions in different years.

In the prehistoric Sierra, each animal found its own home in the environment most suited to it. Each had its own favorite zone, its own range, where the food was nutritious and plentiful. Some stayed within a limited area, while for many others, life was a nomadic affair, following the best food sources with the seasons. In winter, mule deer followed the new grasses that grew much of the season in the low foothills, then traveled up through the forest meadows in summer and into the alpine zone in autumn to eat tender grasses and willow leaves until the first big snowfall.

The soil in the High Sierra was salt-poor and the streams were low in minerals, so animals that preferred the highlands had to adapt. Some rodents, such as the chickaree, or red squirrel, that were normally vegetarian ate meat in the highest regions in order to obtain sufficient salt. Other

Sierra mule deer —Courtesy Tom Marshall, County Bear Originals

animals and birds searched out fire ashes or mud at mineral springs to satisfy their cravings.

For approximately the past 1,000 years, the southern Sierra Nevada has contained five basic life zones. Some of the larger mammals live in, or often visit, more than one or even all of them.

Foothill Belt: On the west side of the southern Sierra, the foothills range from 1,000 to 4,000 feet in elevation. It is a zone that nurtures many species. Although summer heat and water shortages are seasonal absolutes, for most of the year food supplies are plentiful and varied, with nutritious nuts and grasses, immense insect populations, fish, and small animal resources. Cover from predators and numerous nesting sites make it a preferred zone for both year-round residents and migratory visitors.

The foothills region is a permanent home to acorn eaters such as gray and ground squirrels, wood rats, acorn woodpeckers, scrub jays,

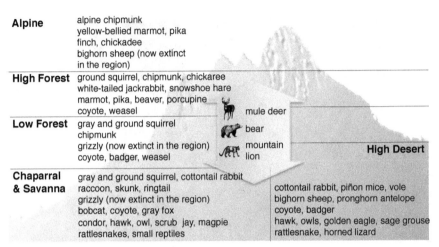

Alpine	alpine chipmunk
	yellow-bellied marmot, pika
	finch, chickadee
	bighorn sheep (now extinct
	in the region)

High Forest	ground squirrel, chipmunk, chickaree
	white-tailed jackrabbit, snowshoe hare
	marmot, pika, beaver, porcupine
	coyote, weasel

mule deer

Low Forest	gray and ground squirrel
	chipmunk
	grizzly (now extinct in the region)
	coyote, badger, weasel

bear

mountain lion

High Desert

Chaparral & Savanna	gray and ground squirrel, cottontail rabbit
	raccoon, skunk, ringtail
	grizzly (now extinct in the region)
	bobcat, coyote, gray fox
	condor, hawk, owl, scrub jay, magpie
	rattlesnakes, small reptiles

cottontail rabbit, piñon mice, vole
bighorn sheep, pronghorn antelope
coyote, badger
hawk, owls, golden eagle, sage grouse
rattlesnake, horned lizard

Sierra Nevada animal zones —Illustration by Laile DiSilvestro

magpies, cottontail rabbits, and some bears and deer. Birds, mice, and rats depend on its vast supply of seeds and insects. The abundance of prey makes it a favored territory for predatory bobcats, rattlesnakes, hawks, condors, and owls. Omnivores, including jays, raccoons, ringtail cats, skunks, gray foxes, and coyotes, have almost unlimited choices, from nuts and berries to eggs, nestlings, rodents, reptiles, and amphibians—whatever suits their particular taste. During the summer, both full-time residents and visitors settle along rivers and streams or in riparian woodlands.

The foothills' chaparral area also sustains a varied animal population. The hillsides covered with dense shrubs made entry difficult for large predators, providing a protective home for many small birds and mammals. Most of these prey animals also have drab gray and brown coloration that makes them difficult to see. The chaparral region is one of the most fire-prone vegetation zones in the Sierra. While wildfires may pose an immediate threat to animals, its occupants in fact depend on fires to renew food plants that have become shriveled and depleted of nutrients in the dry environment. In prehistoric times, the brown grizzly bear made the chaparral area its stomping grounds.

Forest Belt, Yellow Pine Zone: The lower portions of the forest belt contain animals that thrive in 2,500- to 8,000-foot elevations in the southern Sierra Nevada. Their mixed coniferous and broadleaf trees

Grizzly bears were dominant creatures in the High Sierra region in prehistoric times. They ranged from the foothills up through the forest regions during different times of the year. Grizzlies no longer exist in California. —Courtesy Domen Blenkus, istockphotos

hold thick understories of herbs and shrubs. With an abundance of food, shelter, good climate, and water all year long, these forests support the largest variety of animals in the Sierra. They are home to black bears, mule deer, mountain lions, badgers, weasels, gray and ground squirrels, chipmunks, lizards, toads, frogs, salamanders, and various snakes.

In winter months, some lower forest animals, such as mountain lions, deer, bears, and several species of birds, move down into the foothill chaparral and oak forests. However, the majority remain in the yellow pine belt, with their populations reaching a peak during spring migrations in late June. In summer, they adapt to heat and drought. Many hunt at night; some migrate upslope; the California ground squirrel and western spadefoot toad go into estivation, a torpid state, as long as the heat wave lasts.

Golden mantled ground squirrel —Courtesy Elsvander Gun, istockphotos

Forest Belt, Lodgepole Pine/Red Fir Zone: In 4,000- to 10,000-foot-elevation forests, the animal communities become more selective. Many move freely from zone to zone as the seasons change, but some stay throughout the winter. In snow country, marmots, ground squirrels, chipmunks, and western jumping mice hibernate. Those black bears that don't move to lower elevations sleep heavily in winter dens. Other year-round residents stay active through the winter. Pikas eat stored plants they have tucked between rocks on talus slopes. Chickarees live in tree cavities and dig in the snow to find the caches of cones and mushrooms they buried in the fall. Deer mice store food in burrows they dig in the snow. Pocket gophers survive in underground burrows and eat the roots and plant stems that line them. Predators hunt for mountain beavers, porcupines, shrews, white-tailed jackrabbits, snowshoe hares, and weasels.

Fire presents a special problem in the forest zones, for a burn there can last weeks or even months. Larger animals and most birds flee or move to the cooler, moister, less flammable north-facing slopes. Smaller animals go underground, into deep rock crevices and outcroppings, or beneath logs and tree trunks that still have living bark. An amazing number survive. After the fire is over, rich new growth appears and seeds exposed in deep litter provide food for small birds and rodents.

The tiny tailless pika inhabits the Sierra's upper forests and rocky alpine areas. Its existence depends on fickle weather patterns. —Courtesy Twildlife, Dreamstime

Alpine Belt: The alpine world above 10,000 feet escapes the threat of fire, but food and shelter are in short supply all year. In spite of harsh winters and sparse food sources, rosy finches, bighorn sheep, pikas, yellow-bellied marmots, alpine chipmunks, and a variety of migrating

The gray wolf once lived throughout the southern Sierra forests. It was often a major character in prehistoric legends and tales. —Courtesy Fred Reimer

bird species all inhabit the highlands. In winter, most alpine birds migrate to lower elevations, but some, such as finches and chickadees, remain, finding shelter under rocks and bushes during storms. The bighorn sheep scratch up feed from below the snow, moving downhill only in the most extreme conditions. Pikas, marmots, and chipmunks survive in underground burrows and cavities, emerging when the snow begins to melt. After especially long winters, many never emerge, having run out of food before spring came.

Piñon-Sagebrush Belt: The piñon and sagebrush areas that rim the east-side deserts are filled with animal life, for sagebrush scrub provides both food and shelter all year long. The winters can be cold, but the region's porous soils seldom hold snow very long. A wide range of plants provide leaves, flowers, barks, and berries, and in the spring, grasses and forbs are abundant. Although lack of water can be a problem and most annual plants die by midsummer, animals have learned to adapt. As in the chaparral areas of the west-side foothills, many species reduce heat absorption and moisture loss by adapting light coloration; others become nocturnal. Those that cannot obtain sufficient moisture from the foods they eat may move to nearby streams.

Many full-time residents of the piñon-sagebrush belt, such as mule deer, bighorn sheep, antelopes, and pronghorns, resided here in prehistoric times, dining on horsebrush, bitterbrush, sage, wild buckwheat, Mormon tea, needle grasses, and a variety of herbs. With them came horned lizards, speckled rattlesnakes, sage grouse, cottontail rabbits, piñon mice, and voles from the Great Basin deserts. Predators such as hawks, owls, golden eagles, and coyotes also made this region their home.

Most of the Sierra Nevada animals from late prehistoric times survive to this day. The grizzly bear, gray wolf, jaguar, pronghorn, and bison were among the prehistoric species that did not survive in the High Sierra region; some did not survive at all. When humans arrived and disrupted the balance of their world, they gradually disappeared.

5. Human Settlement

THE CREATION OF MAN
A Central Sierra Miwok Tale

After the coyote had finished all the work of making the world and the animal creatures, he called a council of them to deliberate on the creation of man. They sat down in an open space in the forest, all in a circle, with the mountain lion at the head.

The lion was the first to speak. He declared he should like to see man created with a mighty voice like himself. The grizzly bear said the man ought to have prodigious strength, and move about silently but very swiftly if necessary, and be able to grip his prey without making a noise.

The buck said the man would look very foolish unless he had a magnificent pair of antlers on his head to fight with. The mountain sheep protested that there was no sense in having such antlers, branching every which way and getting caught in thickets. If the man had rolled-up horns, they would enable him to butt a great deal harder.

When it was the coyote's turn to speak, he declared that these were the stupidest speeches he had ever heard. Every one of the

"The animals could not agree, and the council broke up in disaccord. Each animal set to work to make a man according to his own ideas." —The Giant Ke'-lok, from *Myths Depicted by Demming and Hittle*, C. Hart Merriam, courtesy Bancroft Library, UC Berkley

animals wanted to make the man like himself. As for him, he knew he was not the best animal that could be made, but he could make one better than himself or any other. Of course, the man would have to be like himself in having four legs, each with five fingers. He could have a voice like the lion, but need not roar with it. The coyote was in favor of making the man's feet nearly like the grizzly's, and without a tail, for he had learned from experience that a tail was only a harbor for fleas.

The buck's eyes were good, perhaps better than his own. The man should be hairless like the fish, for hair was a burden most of the year. His claws ought to be as long as the eagle's for holding things. But after all that, there was no other animal that had wit enough to supply the man; the coyote should be obliged, therefore, to make him cunning and crafty like himself.

The debate continued. The beaver thought the man should have a broad, flat tail. The owl wanted to give him wings, but the mole said that was folly, for the man would certainly bump his head against the sky and burn his eyes out for getting too close to the sun—better to have no eyes at all and just burrow in the cool, soft earth. The mouse squeaked out that the man should have eyes, of course, so he could see what he was eating.

The animals could not agree, and the council broke up in disac-cord. Each animal set to work to make a man according to his own ideas. Taking a lump of earth, each one commenced molding it like himself. But the coyote began to make one like what he had described in the council. Night fell before anyone had finished his model, and they all lay down and went to sleep—all but the cunning coyote, who stayed awake and worked on his model all night. Then he went around and poured water on the other animals' models to spoil them.

In the morning, the coyote finished his model and, long before the others could make new models, he gave it life. Thus it was that man was made by the coyote.

—Adapted from Stephen Powers, *Tribes of California.*[1]

IT TOOK ALMOST 2 MILLION YEARS for humans to find their way to the High Sierra region. The process required millennia of physical adaptations and migrations from Africa to Asia, to Europe, and finally into North America.

The people who migrated into Europe and northern Asia remained there throughout the northern continental glacial period, from 300,000 to 250,000 years ago. They adjusted to the cold by eating the fat of animals, building fires,

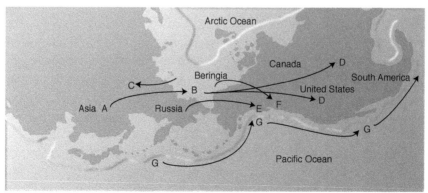

Migration routes of early prehistoric peoples who came into North America from Asia (A-B) and Russia (E) over land routes created when low seas were filled with sediment during the ice ages. Most of the migrants spread out over the Americas (F, D); others sailed along the Pacific shoreline (G); and some returned to Asia (C). The land reclaimed from the sea, now called Beringia, is shown in lighter relief over today's continents.
—Illustration by Laile DiSilvestro

and using animal skins and furs for clothing and blankets. Eventually the cold climate encouraged more migrations, for as the northern oceans froze, they captured and held more water, exposing ground surface along which people could travel to new lands. The migrations came in fits and starts, with different hunting groups exploring the new lands as climatic conditions allowed, expanding their ranges with each expedition and eventually settling father and farther away from their place of origin.

About 85,000 years ago, during a relatively warm interglacial period, hunters in northern Asia moved far into the Arctic north to pursue reindeer. Some 5,000 years later, an extreme cold spell exposed many of the world's continental shelves, and a land bridge emerged at what is now the Bering Strait, between Asia and North America. Discoveries of hand axes and stone tools dating to more than 20,000 years ago indicate that Asian hunters migrated over the Bering land bridge to North America. They continued their migrations south and east, along dry corridors through ice fields into warmer regions. Evidence shows that they also came in boats, tracing the Pacific coastline and developing settlements along its shores.

As the climate of North America continued to warm, fertile ecosystems flourished. The human population pursued the abundant food sources through the central plains and into the eastern and southern regions of what is now the United States. A few moved into present California.

It is unknown who the first groups to discover California were. They may have been the Hokans and the Numic-speaking peoples. The Hokans were a linguistically related people from northern Athabaskan cultures who had settled in the northwest areas of Canada, Washington, and Oregon. The Numic peoples are believed to have migrated south along the Pacific coast to the American Southwest, Mexico, and South America. However, it wasn't until around 13,000 years ago that both groups created settlements in California. Hokan communities appeared on the shores of Tulare Lake, in the area of present-day Fresno, and along the northern and southern coasts, while the Numic speakers moved up from the Southwest to settle in southern California, around Lake Mojave and the Kern River.

In some ways, the west coast interior was not an easy place to inhabit at that time. It was covered with mountains, broad deserts, and large bodies of water to circumnavigate. Some mammoths and other large game animals still roamed, but for the most part the western lands held smaller game such as scattered herds of elk, deer, and antelope, which were more difficult to hunt.

The first people to enter the Sierra Nevada settled in valleys at the edge of the foothills, where water abounded and plant and animal life flourished. —Courtesy Tom Marshall, Country Bear Originals

On the other hand, the lowlands of California offered a life of relative plenty at the end of the last (Pleistocene) ice age, with a moderate climate that was cool and moist, perfect for the habitation of man. By 12,000 years ago, the earliest known full-time California residents were gathering shellfish by the ocean, foraging plants in the Central Valley, fishing in its lakes, and gathering nuts in the lower foothills. Over the next few millennia, hunting became secondary to fishing, trapping, and gathering.

While people thrived in the central valleys, the High Sierra was visited infrequently during these early prehistoric times, for the range presented many problems. Earthquakes shook large areas. Volcanoes erupted along its sides. Its higher reaches held lingering glaciers and were covered with snow for months. Its forests held limited forage for humans, and hunting required long treks.

CENTURIES PASSED FROM THE TIME these early migrants first settled in California to the habitation of the higher elevations of the Sierra Nevada. By 10,000 years ago, high summer camps began to appear, perhaps because of a change in the weather. The cool, wet climate became drier. The Sierra glaciers had nearly vanished, the large lake systems to the east and west of the mountains had diminished, and the lower streams on which man's first settlements developed grew smaller or disappeared. Whole communities began to move, seeking the life-giving waters and food resources that the mountains and upper foothills provided.

Eventually, the summer camps turned into permanent settlements. Two of the earliest villages were at Kennedy Meadows, on the South Fork of the Kern River, and Long Valley, north of the Owens Valley. Both became long-term communities, inhabited from about 8,500 years ago into historic times. Another permanent settlement was established near the Kings River at the 7,000-foot-elevation Balsam Meadow, settled as early as 7,000 years ago. During this time, the number of summer hunting and trading camps increased along what is now the Pacific Crest Trail.

From about 6,400 to 2,900 years ago, during an extremely warm period in southern California, the foothills of the southern Sierra and the lower canyons of the Kern River also experienced the full-time occupation of man. One

One of the earliest permanent settlements was in Kennedy Meadows, on the South Fork of the Kern River. —From author's files

community developed below the eastern Sierra scarp at Little Lake, which was a salt grass meadow then, filled with marshes, ponds, and wildlife. It was a perfect area for hunting and gathering, with its elevation high enough to provide cooling summer breezes, yet low enough to gather warmth from a winter sun. A large community also developed on the North Fork of the Kern, at the confluence of Osa and Soda creeks, around 3,150 years ago. Below it, another large hamlet, now called Holit, was settled just north of Bull Run Creek.

Each time the climate changed, people adapted, moving up- or downslope. Some time around 3,500 to 2,600 years ago, a cool spell created colder summers and lingering winter snows, so some Sierra settlers may have returned to the lowlands. But a new situation arose. A group of immigrants who spoke the Penutian languages, a group possibly descended from the Ob River area of northwestern Siberia, began displacing the earlier Hokan cultures. Just as the original peoples had come in several waves, so the new cultures came over a period of hundreds of years, gradually settling into the best living areas in the central portions of California. As the overall population grew, habitable land became an important commodity. Many higher Sierra communities remained occupied year-round, and boundary disputes became more common.

The different cultures met, perhaps fought, intermarried, and integrated, until many of the old ways and traditions disappeared. Throughout a period of 2,500 years, new tools and technologies developed, some that the Penutian immigrants may have brought with them—abalone fish hooks, awls, needles, and harpoons; stone mortars and pestles to replace cumbersome milling stones; and eventually, the bow and arrow. It was a time of transition and change, of adaptation and melding, of learning a better way of life.

During the drought periods of 900 and 650 years ago, populations throughout the High Sierra region became smaller and more dispersed, possibly due to a lack of resources. Occupation of some villages in the lower foothills became sporadic, while elevations above 5,000 feet saw an increase in seasonal camps. Entire communities evidently moved higher into the mountains for relief from the heat and drought.

In spite of the ups and downs, California seems to have been as desirable in ancient times as it continues to be today. By the time Europeans made their entrance, it already was one of the most densely populated areas on the continent north of Mexico, supporting a variety of peoples. With each migration, the diversity of languages increased, until at least sixty-four to eighty different languages were spoken, each with several separate dialects.

By late prehistoric times, after 1,000 years ago, the original Hokans and Numic-speaking peoples had broken into several linguistically distinct groups. The southern Sierra Hokan people integrated with Penutian immigrants and developed the Miwok and Yokuts cultures. The Numic people divided into Uto-Aztecan groupings of the Southwest and Great Basin areas, with cultural offshoots of Tubatulabal, Paiute, and Monache in the southern Sierra. Each of these larger tribal entities subdivided into smaller cultural and familial

As the original California people proliferated, they broke into many subgroups that claimed their own territories, developed their own languages, and created their own cultures. —Adapted from map by A. L. Kroeber in R. F. Heizer's Languages, Territories, and Names of California Indian Tribes

groupings that occupied distinct areas of the High Sierra region, spoke their own dialects, and developed their own cultural practices and traditions: the central and the southern Sierra Miwok, fifteen or more Sierra foothill Yokuts groups, three Tubatulabal groups, several western Monache bands, the eastern Monache, and the Owens Valley Paiute; all had separate identities.

THERE IS NO ONE WAY TO DESCRIBE prehistoric life in the Sierra Nevada. Ten thousand years of human adaptation created many different and changing ways of life. Still, archaeological evidence and anthropological study have allowed us to piece together a picture of these early Californians that shows the similarities as well as differences among them.

In many ways, all later prehistoric southern Sierra people practiced similar survival strategies and daily living routines. They were hunters and gatherers, dependent on plant resources augmented with game for their basic diet. They exploited the same basic resources within specific territories using similar methods and tools—digging roots, picking berries, harvesting grasses, gathering nuts and seeds; collecting insects, grubs, and worms to eat; corraling, spearing, or netting fish, or paralyzing them with poison. Through the centuries, their hunting technology progressed from darts, spears, and atlatls to include bows and arrows, which they used along with trapping, spearing, and driving game into enclosures. Most relied on the same animals for meat. Fish, rabbit, squirrel, and deer were their mainstays, supplemented with wild sheep, bear, pronghorn antelope, and smaller mammals and birds. Every group used fire, not only for warmth and cooking, but also to clear the land, to promote new growth, and to drive prey to hunting fields.

All groups also had comparable processes and devices for collecting, preparing, preserving, and storing food. Their food preparation transitioned from a predominant use of portable metates and pounding rocks to widespread use of bedrock mortars and pestles. They created food caches and made specialized baskets for gathering, carrying, food preparation, and storage. They leached acids out of acorns and buckeye nuts, ground them into meal, and cooked the meal in water to create mushes, soups, and unleavened cakes. Food was cooked with hot rocks in tightly woven baskets, in clay or steatite bowls over fire, or put directly into beds of hot ashes and coals.

While they spoke different languages and dialects, most groups mixed with their neighbors, and many intermarried. At times, they shared hunting grounds and cooperated in hunting expeditions. They traded with one another often and utilized various forms of money, such as chunks of steatite and clamshells, with systems of counting into the hundreds. Each group sent members out to explore and find new trails, campsites, and hunting areas, so that, according to ethnologist Albert Elsasser, "in aboriginal times in the Sierra Nevadan province, little or no land, even at the highest elevations, was unknown to the Indians."[2]

The various peoples also shared common ground culturally. They played and sang music and created art in their basketry, clothing, and body decorations. Gambling, hand games, and field games were much the same. All indulged in tobacco use and encouraged its growth in some manner. Having no written languages, storytelling was both a form of entertainment and an important means of teaching.

Similarities also existed in their spiritual beliefs and rituals. Every group had some type of puberty ceremony and a mourning ceremony for the dead. All had creation stories and myths about the origins of the natural elements

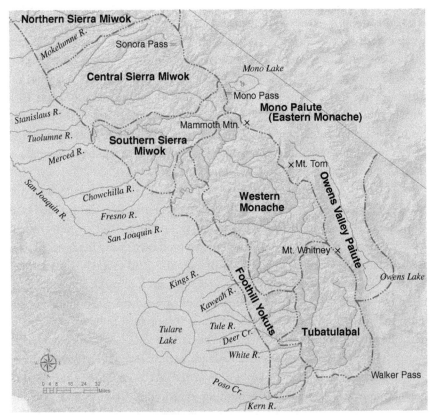

Five tribal groups settled in the southern Sierra region, each with its own subdivisions, dialects, and cultures.

that were central to their lives. There was a universal belief in the importance of dreams and in the power of spirits and ghosts. Shamans of several varieties, and especially healing doctors, were important to each group. Herbal medicines were used everywhere.

Even with all the commonalities of the High Sierra region's people, there were also many differences that defined each group. Those differences developed from variations in background, environment, leadership, and outside cultural influences—the basis for each group's own cultural identity.

PART II

6. The Tubatulabal

CONTEST TO DETERMINE DIVISION OF LABOR
A Tubatulabal Tale

Before Indians lived on this earth, there were many kinds of animals and birds living here. All of them were men animals. There were no women animals, it is said. These men—Chicken, Hawk, Sparrow Hawk, Mountain Lion, Bear, Coyote, and the chief, Eagle—hunted rabbits every day. When they tired of hunting rabbits they went to hunt deer in the mountains. In the mountains the hunters saw smoke rising from a peak. They said, "Perhaps somebody is living over there. Let's send somebody over there to find out." They chose Roadrunner because he could travel fast.

On the mountain there were many women creatures: Eagle Woman, Coyote Woman, Mountain Lion Woman, and many others. There were no men, only women there. All of them were sitting around a big pit mortar bed with lots of mortar holes in it, pounding piñons. Roadrunner saw the women there and they called to him to come in. Each of the women gave Roadrunner a little bag of food for each man at the camp. "In three days we will come over to your camp," they told him.

In three days' time the women came. Each one had a bow and arrow. Each of the women went to the house of the man of her own kind. The next day, all the men went hunting and all the women went to grind acorns and chia. The hunters returned in the evening, and the women had their supper waiting.

The following day, the women told the men, "We are going to go hunting now. You men go and grind some acorns." When the women returned in the evening each of them had a deer. Some of the men had finished their work, but others were still at the mortar holes grinding acorns. At sundown, Coyote was still at the pit leaching acorn meal, and he was angry. Coyote said, "Those women have bows and arrows and they hunt; they send us over to the pit mortars to grind acorns. That is not right. I think women better handle the mortar and pestle. It's a woman's job, not a man's. Tomorrow we are

"I think women better handle the mortar and pestle. It's a woman's job, not a man's." —Woman grinding nuts, courtesy F. Latta and A. Barr, from Kern River historical reenactment, Tulare County Office of Education

going to shoot at a target. If the women win, they can handle the arrow. If we win, we can keep on hunting and the women will handle the pestle all the time."

When daylight came Coyote set up a target. The animal couples lined up in a double column. All the men and women shot and missed the target, until Mountain Lion and his wife had their turn. As Mountain Lion's wife shot, Coyote said, "Break, bowstring! Break, bowstring! Break, bowstring!" Mountain Lion Woman's string broke and her arrow dropped beside the target. But Mountain Lion hit the target right in the center. So the women lost and the men won.

"Now, all right! You women handle the mortar; we men will handle the arrows. We are men," said Coyote, it is said.

—Adapted from Erminie Voegelin, *Tubatulabal Ethnography*.[1]

THE TUBATULABAL (pronounced too-BOT-oo-LA-bal) may have been the first people to make the southern Sierra Nevada their permanent territory. Their ancient name was Tubat, meaning "pine-nut eaters." Ask a Tubatulabal how long their people were in the Sierra and he or she would answer, "forever."[2]

Descendants of the Uto-Aztecan peoples of the southern desert regions, the Tubatulabal separated from the Numic-speaking Shoshonean people of the Great Basin area about 3,000 years ago. Isolated in the southern foothills surrounding the Kern River and Deer Creek drainages, they never integrated with the Shoshoneans to their east nor with the western Penutian-speaking immigrants who later encroached on their territory. They were proud of their distinct identity and disdained the cultural intermixing neighboring tribes engaged in.

There were three bands of Tubatulabal, each with its own headman.[3] The most populated band, the Pahkanapil, built their winter villages on the South Fork of the Kern River where extensive floodplain meadows, two large lakes, and marshlands spread. The Palagewan inhabited the spring- and stream-fed basins along the North Fork of the Kern. The Toloim, or Bankalachi as the neighboring Yokuts called them, had most of their permanent villages on the west side of the Sierra along Deer Creek. All the permanent winter villages of the three bands lay in the comfortable 2,500- to 3,200-foot elevation levels on dry ridges or plateaus, close to good water and fuel sources.

Over the centuries, the Tubatulabal developed a unique variation of the Uto-Aztecan languages. Unlike the languages of surrounding groups, theirs most often ended in consonant sounds. According to scholar Edward Winslow Gifford, both the Tubatulabal and their southern neighbors, the Kawaiisu, used individual names, terms, and suffixes to denote place in family, marriage connections, and relationship to the dead. Thus a woman could be called *abu* by her children if none of them had died, but *umu* after the death of one. She, along with her brothers and sisters, was *tumu* to her mother,

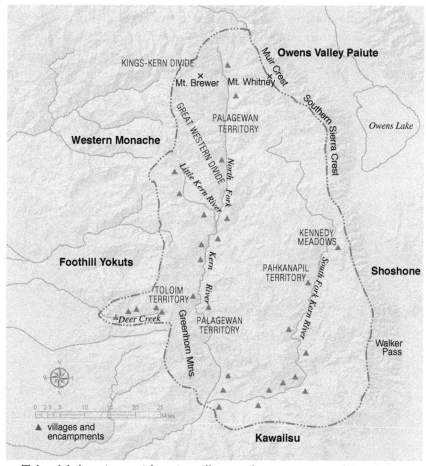

Tubatulabal territory with major villages and encampments —Adapted from Erminie Voegelin, Anthropological Records 2:1, UC Berkeley

father, aunts, uncles, and male cousins. She was *kutei* to an older sister or female cousin; *anociwan* to her father's second wife; *agistbin* to her daughter's child; *utsu* to her mother's mother or mother's sister; *hoki* to a grandchild after her own death.[4]

While the dialects of each band varied in small ways, the Tubatulabal considered themselves one culture. They socialized and intermarried. They joined together for rabbit drives, hunting and gathering expeditions, feasts, dances, games, and mourning ceremonies. They traded dried venison, fish, and other staples and lent clamshell money to one another without charging interest. The bands also occasionally joined forces in battles with neighboring Yokuts, Kawaiisu, and Coso communities.

Taken as a whole, the Tubatulabal territory extended over 1,300 square miles from the western Sierra foothills to the edges of the eastern desert. It covered a forty-mile-long stretch up both branches of the Kern to their headwaters along the eastern crest of the Sierra, including the regions surrounding Mt. Whitney. Every life zone was represented within these

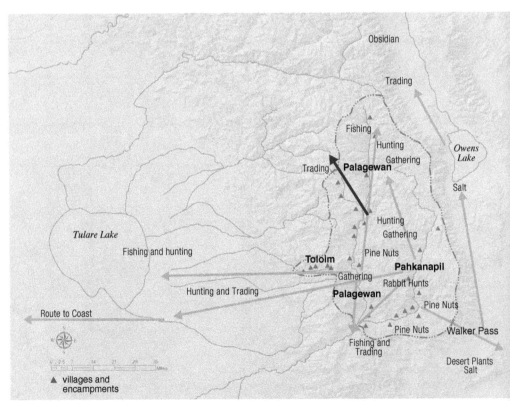

Seasonal migrations and activity zones in Tubatulabal territory

Palagewan village site on the Kern River's North Fork —From author's files

indefinite boundaries, of which two-thirds lay in the summer hunting and gathering grounds of the High Sierra. Even in drought years, the Tubatulabal could always find food.

The Palagewan Tubatulabal, on the North Fork of the Kern River, enjoyed the most diverse resources. Their winter villages were surrounded by piñon and Utah juniper forests. Their summer camps stretched from Jeffrey pines up into fir, incense cedar, hemlock, sugar pine, and lodgepole pine forests of the Main Fork, at 7,000- to 8,000-foot elevations. There they hunted, fished, and gathered bulbs and berries.

The villages of the Pahkanapil, on the South Fork of the Kern, took advantage of the resources of their meadows, wetlands, lakes, and surrounding piñon, juniper, and mountain mahogany forests all year long. In summer they camped in the Jeffrey and lodgepole pine forests at the headwaters of the South Fork, but they often joined the Palagewan in hunting and gathering expeditions up the Main Fork, making camps along the eastern crest of the Southern Sierra.

The forested upper Kern Canyon on the North Fork had several summer occupation sites used by both the Palagewan and Pahkanapil. —From author's files

The environment of the Toloim band, on the west side of the Tubatulabal territory, was more self-contained. The Toloim built their winter villages almost entirely in the oak-covered foothill regions of Deer Creek, where year-round forage was close at hand. Their summer camps were in the oak, pine, fir, and giant sequoia forests of the nearby 5,000- to 7,000-foot-high Greenhorn Mountain spur, where hunting was good, and highly desired black-oak acorns were abundant.

TUBATULABAL WOMEN ENJOYED RIGHTS AND PRIVILEGES unknown in most prehistoric California communities. They had an equal voice in all decisions that affected family life. Their kinship ties were honored; mothers and grandmothers named the babies without following paternal lines. As children, girls were treated no differently than boys, and on reaching adulthood, young women had rights of personal property that no man could take away. Their possessions always passed on to their daughters; they could practice birth control; and they had the right to terminate a pregnancy if they chose, by drinking a pitch or mistletoe concoction. They could become shamans or doctors, and, most unusual among California groups, they had special times during which they could use the community sweathouse.

While women were respected, men and women usually followed the strict division of labor that the mythical people of long ago had decreed. Although the men often shared the daily subsistence chores—child care, food gathering, fire tending—their primary roles were hunting, fishing, trapping, and construction of shelters. They skinned the kill, packed home the meat, tanned the hides, built stone fish corrals, hauled in rock salt, and did most of the duties that required strength.

The women handled the chores that required greater endurance. These included gathering and foraging for foods and medicines; pruning, harvesting, and preserving tobacco leaves; meal preparation and the drying, processing, and storage of food; cleaning; making and mending clothing; weaving baskets; making clay pots; most of the child care; and carrying the household goods when traveling. They often accomplished these chores with a baby in a Y-shaped cradleboard strapped to their backs or stuck in the ground beside them.

Although Tubatulabal women had more rights than those of most Sierra groups, the culture followed hierarchal traditions, and it was the men who held the leadership positions in the villages. Each village, or hamlet, was a winter home base for one extended family consisting of two to six households, each made up of a husband, wife, children, and sometimes other relatives. It was forbidden to marry within one's own village because almost everyone in it was related within a three-generation restriction.

Marriage was mutually consensual. Although a couple's parents did not arrange the union, parental approval was important. Most often, when two young people were attracted to each other, the boy first told his own parents, who visited the girl's family. Assuming the meeting went well, the young man then returned to ask the girl to be his wife. If she accepted his proposal, he returned again with his mother and father, bringing clamshell money as a bride price.[5] If the payment was accepted, the girl's parents gave the young man's parents gifts of food and fine baskets in return. The girl then went to her new husband's village, and the two families held a marriage feast to which both contributed.

Before the wedding, the bride's mother would instruct the girl carefully in wifely protocol regarding her future in-laws. She was to speak sparingly to her mother- and father-in-law; to address them always in the plural and turn aside if she met them on a trail; and to generally treat them with an exaggerated deference and respect. After the marriage, it was typically the wife who moved to her new husband's village, but if the couple agreed it was more advantageous for themselves and for their children, a husband might live in his wife's village for several years or even permanently. Usually, however, children grew up in their father's village. Thus a boy generally lived in the same community that his father, grandfather, and all the male members of his family had lived in for at least four generations.

WHEN A YOUNG TUBATULABAL WOMAN LEFT HER FAMILY, she took with her all the items she would need as a wife, carried on her back in a burden basket. The large, conical basket was made of twined willow root, yucca root, and deer grass that had been stiffened with soaproot juice. This basket could hold up to 200 pounds. To ease the weight on her back, she wore a tumpline fitted across a coiled basketry cap that sat over the singed bangs on her forehead.

Burden baskets were used by all prehistoric Sierra Nevada women. The baskets' forms varied according to what was going to be carried. —Courtesy Tulare County Museum

In the burden basket would be some clothes: a double-aproned, tanned deerskin skirt with a deer-hoof dew-claw fringe around the bottom, to be worn on special occasions; a buckskin breechclout; a fur vest, often made of bearskin; a rabbit-skin shoulder blanket; and tall buckskin boots for cold weather.

Accessories might include necklaces, bracelets, and earrings of white clamshell disks and steatite beads; pigment powders to paint her face; and a special cylindrical shell nose ornament, worn through her septum for dances.

Also in the basket were the tools and materials the woman would need for her primary work of food gathering and preparation. These might include coils of milkweed twine and hemp cordage; a fire-starting stick made of cottonwood roots; hot-rock lifters; and a looped-stick mush stirrer. An obsidian knife, a shell spoon, an oak digging stick, various awls, and bone needles were essentials. The woman might also carry a soaproot hairbrush, ground soaproot shampoo, and alkali powder for lice.

On the outside of the burden basket, several smaller baskets made of deer grass, redbud shoots, and willow or yucca roots would probably hang. One or two of them would be for boiling acorn and pine-nut mush, accomplished by placing hot stones along with meal and water inside the basket. Others might include a sifting basket that doubled as a small tray; another tray used for parching chia and grass seeds with live embers; and one made of tule reeds, used in the drying of reed sugar. Other items hanging on the burden basket might be a mortar hopper, usually made from an old cooking basket with the bottom cut out; basketry ladles and seed beaters; a water bottle made leak-proof and sweet tasting with a covering of red earth and piñon pine pitch; and a bottle-necked basket in which strings of clamshell money was collected.

Among the articles inside her burden basket, the heaviest, but most important in early times was a portable metate (a stone mortar, or grinding slab), shaped to the woman's individual liking and used in conjunction with a mano (hand stone) for grinding nuts into flour. This tool would be used virtually every day of a woman's life.

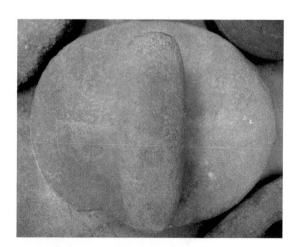

Portable grinding slabs were used throughout prehistoric times for meal preparation when traveling. —Courtesy Tulare County Museum

It was a woman's duty to devote herself to the well-being of her family and her village. If her husband was good to her, a Tubatulabal woman would work hard to take special care of him. She would serve him his meals first, cheer him in his field games, and sing and chant behind him to help his luck when he gambled in hand games.

When a Tubatulabal couple established their own home, it was the job of the husband and his family to provide it. This would usually be a small, domed dwelling built to last two to four years and just large enough for two people and maybe a baby or two. It would have a sweet-smelling thatched grass covering, clay-plastered brush walls, and green tule mats on the floor, with rabbit-skin blankets for winter. The dome had a smoke hole in the center for the recessed fireplace, which was used mainly for cooking in winter.

As the family grew, the men of the village might build a larger rectangular house for them. These larger homes often had one wall that could be raised in the summer to let the cool mountain breezes in. Some had a flat, shading canopy outside too, and a windbreak fence made of rocks or piled brush. No matter what their wealth or position, the family lived and worked outdoors most of the time.

In all the communities of the Kern, women enjoyed a high status and held important roles as teachers. They taught the children the customs, manners, and taboos of Tubatulabal culture. They admonished them not to talk about others, not to stare at people, not to be stingy; to always give visitors food; to avoid showing anger so you would not grow old too quickly; and to treat the old people well. During long winter evenings, the elder women of the village told stories of the old animal people, tales that depicted the morals of Tubatulabal society. Older women also tattooed the young girls' chins and arms and pierced their earlobes and septums so the girls could adorn the piercings with strings, painted sticks, reed tubes, feathers, and shell cylinders, a practice not followed by boys or men. All women and girls painted themselves and each other with charcoal and red and white minerals before dances and ceremonies.

Traditionally, it was the women who gathered medicinal herbs and administered many of the everyday remedies. One cure entailed swallowing red ants wrapped in balls of eagle-down to alleviate chills and fever. Only when serious illness or accidents occurred did they seek the counsel and help of a bear or rattlesnake shaman, to intervene at the source of the problem; a weather shaman to change a weather pattern that may be creating the conditions of accidents or illness; or a curing shaman who could exorcise the offending spirits creating the illness.

A good Tubatulabal woman always followed strict meat and salt taboos during her menstrual period and when she was pregnant. Expectant mothers increased their own workload to assure a healthy child and easy delivery. When a pregnant woman went into labor, her husband dug a shallow three-foot trench as a birthing bed, in which he built a fire and laid slabs of stone, then dirt, then woven mats. After the birth, mother and newborn would lie on the heated bed for six days to heal. The mother pulled out the afterbirth herself, wrapped it in buckskin, and saved it for her own mother to bury outside her home. About one week after birth, the child's maternal grandmother, and sometimes its grandfather, named the baby, often for a relative who had died at least two to three years earlier.

Children's days were filled with activities that emulated the work of their elders and taught them specific skills. Girls learned how to work with clay, make clothing, find herbs, gather food, dig roots and bulbs, and prepare meals. Boys practiced shooting with bows and arrows scaled to their size. They learned how to track and hunt small game and how to fish. For fun, youngsters practiced string tricks resembling cat's cradle and figures of mythical animal beings. Toys included clay dolls; toy bows and arrows; spinning acorn tops; bone whistles; and acorn buzzers that made a sound when a string was pulled through them. One toy, a wooden bull roarer, made a loud roaring sound that could be heard at long distances.

Growing up, both boys and girls often created a special lifelong "chum" relationship with a friend. According to ethnologist Erminie Voegelin, "Two unrelated boys or two unrelated girls, when about eight years old, often assumed a chum relationship; boys exchanged bows and arrows; girls bracelets; this relationship lasted into adult life. Chums used each other's belongings freely, lived at each other's homes . . . went out hunting and to get wood together."[6]

After they reached puberty, girls and boys were encouraged to participate in jimson-drinking rites to guarantee a long and healthy life. Five to six boys and girls were taken to a sweathouse on a winter evening to stay for three nights and days. An elder male guided the group in following a strict diet and gave them emetics to induce vomiting. On the third evening, the man gave the adolescents a jimson concoction that caused them to fall into a stupor for several hours. Those who experienced visions then fasted an entire day and refrained from eating meat or grease for two months.

Every day at sunrise, the entire village ate breakfast together—usually dried meat dipped in acorn mush. The evening meal might be mush, berries, greens, and fresh meat or fish. Treats included a drink made from roasted blue chia seeds; cakes of sweet sugar from cane plants; and tart chewing gum that Palagewan women made from the sticky white juice of the milkweed, congealed in hot ashes then softened with deer grease.

The Tubatulabal played almost as hard as they worked. Leisure activities included dances, gambling games, and team sports. In summer there were competitive team games of shinny and hoop-and-pole. Shinny, played on a level playing field by both men and women, was somewhat like modern field hockey. Hoop-and-pole, a game much like modern quoits or horseshoes, was played almost daily by men. Guessing games and basket dice might be enjoyed in the sweathouse or under the shade of a spreading oak tree. Basket dice was a woman's game, played on beautifully designed basket trays with five, six, or eight inlaid acorn dice. Scoring rules were intricate.

Most native games throughout the southern Sierra region involved gambling, with bets of shell money placed by both participants and onlookers. Among the most popular forms of gambling were hand games, played in teams of men or women. First, shell bets were exchanged for clay or rock

Games, such as hoop-and-pole, were a favorite pastime for men and boys.
—Courtesy F. Latta and A. Barr, from Kern River historical reenactment, Tulare County Office of Education

counters. When the bets were placed, two "bones," or short sticks, were shuffled from hand to hand under a blanket or a pile of fresh grass by a team member; a guesser from the other team then tried to determine which hand they ended up in. The object was for one team to win all the counters. These hand games could last all night, with the teams singing songs in the belief that the loudest team would win.

FOR THE PAHKANAPIL AND PALAGEWAN BANDS, life depended on a traditional and mostly reliable natural cycle. It started sometime in March, when the geese returned and fishing improved along the lower Kern River. In April, with warmer weather, all the villages converged at the lower gorge of the Kern in a major fishing expedition. Sometimes families visited Tulare Lake as well, to feast on ducks and fish.

In May, after the first high waters of the winter's rain season subsided, the villagers could go out into the lower valleys and foothills to gather grasses, chia seeds, the tender blossoms of yucca plants, and wild clover. They also picked juniper and squawthorn berries, which they boiled and ate or put into their acorn mush. Every other year, they extracted green nuts from new gray-pine cones and ate them on the spot as a treat.

With the warm May weather, members of the two Kern River Tubatulabal bands met for group rabbit hunts in the sagebrush lands, using both noise and fire to drive cottontails and jackrabbits into nets woven from milkweed roots; once caught, the rabbits would be clubbed or shot with arrows. The Pahkanapil also made excursions into the Mojave and Indian Wells desert valleys to gather succulent potatolike yamba bulbs.

June was the month for pruning wild tobacco plants. After pruning the plants once a week for three weeks running, the women gathered the leaves, which each woman claimed for her own family that year. The leaves were sprinkled with pine-nut–infused water, or mixed with greenleaf manzanita. Then they were dried, first wrapped in willow shoots then opened to the sun. Finally, the women pounded and formed them into balls or plugs, ready for trade or for family use.

The men, especially male shamans, smoked the tobacco mixture in wooden or steatite pipes. Both men and women mixed the tobacco with lime, usually from ground clamshells, and chewed the peppery mixture. Or, they made an emetic of tobacco, lime, and water, which they drank in the evening to induce vomiting for a dreamless slumber.

Also in June, the men participated again in rabbit drives and hunted birds and black-tailed deer. The women continued to gather "wild rice," the seeds from wild bunchgrasses, as well as barley, chia, sunflowers, saltbush, sagebrush, and heliotrope. They also dug up the soft new tule roots that grew around springs.

Midsummer was the busiest time of the year. The gathering season was growing short by then, and rush roots, sour-tasting saltgrass, and sweet cane sugar had to be dried for winter use. It became prime fishing season as the runoff of the Sierra winter snows abated. The men built communal fish corrals and harpooned the fish, and the women dried the catches. Prehistoric people in the southern Sierra Nevada practiced various fishing methods, including catching the fish in nets made of native twine or in tule basket traps; fishing with milkweed line and bone hooks; poisoning the water to stupefy the fish; and building fish corrals and weir (fence) traps. The Tubatulabal fish corrals were built in shallow, fast-running water when large numbers of fish were running. These round enclosures were about seven feet in diameter and two to three feet high, with walls built of large stones filled in with willow branches to make them almost waterproof. They also built tule rafts, which were used for lake travel, fishing, and harvesting freshwater mussels from the slow-moving waters at the confluence of the two forks of the Kern and from the two shallow lakes of the South Fork valley.

Tule boats were often used for fishing in calm river areas and lowland lakes. —Courtesy F. Latta and A. Barr, from Kern River historical reenactment, Tulare County Office of Education

Summer was the time for travel as well. Some years, whole villages, which usually included fifteen to twenty extended-family members, went together on trading expeditions across the Greenhorn Mountains into the Yokuts territory. Sometimes they walked far into the vast plains of the lower San Joaquin Valley to trade with the Tuelamni Yokuts for asphaltum or to join in communal antelope drives. Sometimes they trekked all the way to the Pacific coast to indulge in abalone feasts and to trade for valuable seashells.

But the most important trips for all three bands were their summer journeys to the high country. While the Toloim retreated to the upper reaches of the southern Sierra's Greenhorn spur, the Palagewans and Pahkanapil went on summer hunting and gathering expeditions up the Main and South Forks of the Kern River, where they spent as much time as possible camping in the cool air of the higher mountains. There they enjoyed eating all the varieties of grass seeds and greens that sprouted late in snow country: gooseberries, elderberries, and wild strawberries; sugar-pine nuts; cattail roots; mariposa

Tubatulabal summer area —Courtesy Tom Burge, Sequoia National Park archives

lily, camas, and tiger lily bulbs. They also gathered plants for later use, collecting manzanita berries for cider and drying grasses and roots for weaving. The men hunted, skinned, and prepared deer and wild sheep, and fished for golden trout. The women broiled the meat and fish over hot coals or roasted them in hot ashes.

Late August, September, and October were the nut-gathering season. In good harvesting years, the Kern River families went to piñon stands in the eastern Sierra's lower elevations to collect pine nuts. As the gathering season advanced, they moved higher into the Chimney Meadows and Walker Pass areas, storing the piñon nuts in protected caches and, every other year, collecting mature gray-pine nuts to take home. They picked wild grapes in the desert canyons above Indian Wells Valley and gathered blue-oak acorns from trees along the Kern. As autumn drew closer to winter, they visited the Toloim in the Greenhorn Mountains, where the women of all three bands harvested and cached black-oak acorns while the men hunted deer, which had also assembled to eat the nuts.

In autumn villagers fished the quiet pools along the Kern River and its tributaries. Throughout the fall, men also fished from their tule rafts in the area's larger rivers and lakes, and hunted and trapped deer, rabbits, ducks, and

Back from the hunt. Almost all parts of the deer would be utilized for food, clothing, tools, and coverings. —Courtesy F. Latta and A. Barr, from Kern River historical reenactment, Tulare County Office of Education

quail. After drying most of their meat and fish for the winter, Tubatulabal families from all three bands often went on one last trip to the immense Tulare Lake in the San Joaquin Valley, where they visited friendly Yokuts villages and enjoyed their fill of fish and migrating waterfowl.

By the middle of November, the Kern River Tubatulabal had all returned to their winter homes, where they secured their stores of nuts and dried the last of the fish and meat. As winter snows fell in the highlands, some families traveled down to the Mojave Desert to gather salt from the desert lakebeds. Sometimes they turned north and continued to Owens Valley to trade for obsidian pre-forms—pieces of rock suitable for forming into tools—and smaller blanks from which they could carve tools and arrowheads.

As the people of the Kern valleys settled into quiet winter occupations, they visited their piñon and acorn caches often. The young girls learned how to shell acorn nuts with their teeth until their mouths bled. They helped their mothers weave new baskets and mend old ones; fashion new food-processing items such as bowls, grinding stones, and utensils; make new clothing articles and patch old ones; grind meal and tend cooking fires. Their fathers and brothers repaired their dwellings, made new hunting and fishing tools, and joined other men and boys in small-game hunts in the desert. The whole village engaged in hand games and special storytelling sessions held only on winter nights, for at any other time of the year or hour both speakers and listeners courted the danger of snakebites.

Around February, the villagers resumed their trips to nearby lower desert hills and valleys to gather mescal stalks, the tender new pods of Joshua tree yuccas, and various bulbs to augment their diet of dried winter food. So the cycle began again.

APART FROM MINOR VARIATIONS in diet and environmental adaptation, there were more similarities than differences among the Tubatulabal bands. Their cultural views and social customs were basically the same. The Tubatulabal, like all prehistoric Sierra people, had no universal god.[7] Various natural and supernatural forces guided their existence. Many of these were spirits embodied in the forms of animals, which showed themselves to individuals as protective personal "helpers" in dreams and images. Dreams and visions were as important to the Tubatulabal as everyday reality. A wise person paid close attention to them, and when the bad ones came, he tried to blow them away with his breath.

In a life dependent on the vagaries of nature, tuning into the surroundings was crucial. Carefully observing and listening, watching for signs, could mean the difference between life and death. Children grew up with the belief that everything in the Sierra held life. They felt they could communicate with rocks, streams, trees, and animals. They listened for what the barking coyote, the yapping fox, the howling wolf, the crying mountain lion, and the bleating mule deer might be telling them. They learned from the plants which bulbs, leaves, seeds, and roots were edible; from the cliffs and canyons, which rocks might be slippery or ready to fall; from the trees, when the nuts would be ready for harvesting; from the rivers, where the best fishing pools were.

The Toloim learned how to avoid poison oak, thistles, and scratching manzanita as they gathered nuts and berries in the foothill chaparral. They developed a keen sense of smell to detect what the wind carried from afar— what food sources were at hand, whether a grizzly bear was near, or if a lightning fire was approaching. The Palagewan knew which desert plants and water sources enticed deer and pronghorn antelope to the piñon forests. The smell of green tussock grasses and sedges told them of water sources, and the rise of lake waters showed when spring fishing could begin. The "pine-nut eaters"—the Palagewan and Pahkanapil—could tell by the growth of the nuts on the piñon trees how large the fall harvest would be and therefore how much supplemental food they must gather. As fall approached in the summer camps, morning frosts and chill winds alerted the people that it was time to retreat to the lower river valleys.

For prehistoric Sierrans, danger lurked everywhere, not only in the natural world, but in other people and spirits as well. A Tubatulabal was always concerned that someone or something would poison him: a rattlesnake might bite him; his guardian animal spirit might abandon him, or an evil shaman or spirit might capture the soul in his head, and make him sick, or even kill him. One never knew when he might accidentally stumble upon one of the spirit places where the souls of evil shamans, and of animals who had been killed without proper apologies, dwelled.

What an individual did and how he or she did it influenced everything. A man would carefully observe each hunting taboo so he would not be harmed. In molding her clay boiling pots or weaving her work baskets, a woman might carefully work in the same design that her mother always used, to make certain her family's spirit remained with her. It was important for the village to follow daily protocols so that bad things would not happen: everyone eating breakfast together at sunup, and making certain that the day's second meal was held before dark so an evil shaman, ghost, or stranger could not poison the food. When someone died, the rituals of the mourning ceremony had to be followed exactly, for if they were not, the breath of the dead person's soul might not find its way across the eastern mountains to the land of the dead, and it could remain with the living to torment them.

Intertribal conflicts arose occasionally, most often with the Yokuts, even though the Tubatulabal traded, hunted, socialized, and sometimes intermarried with them. In later prehistoric times, the battles were generally over poaching, invasion of food-gathering territories, murder, or an evil shaman's influence. These small wars seldom lasted more than one day, most often taking place in the morning, followed by a quick retreat. Usually the men did not even take food to a battle. The village headmen never participated, but selected a battle leader to be in charge of the raid. No hostages were taken, and there were seldom more than a few casualties, if any, though sometimes women and children were killed in the fighting.

After a fight, the two hostile headmen called a settlement conference. No money or gifts were exchanged, but the differences were talked out. The offending headman promised that the perpetrating incident would not happen again, and both vowed not to fight any more. A joint feast and dancing often followed.

For the Tubatulabal, time did not proceed at a marked rate. There were no months, there were no years. Certain events marked the seasons: the first budding of the willows; the return of waterfowl; the spawning of fish; the ripening of berries, grasses, and tobacco plants; the maturity of acorn crops; snow on the peaks; the migration of birds. Each event was celebrated with dances, ceremonies, food, games, and even clowns.

Life was mostly good for the Tubatulabal people, though it was not an easy life. Theirs was a culture shaped by and adapted to its mountain and high desert environment. It took bonding, cooperation, hard work, and a strong sense of common identity to successfully sustain a way of life over a period of time beyond memory.

7. The Yokuts

THE ANIMAL PEOPLE OBTAIN FIRE
A Yauh'-dahn-chee Yokuts Tale

A long time ago, before the Yauh'-dahn-chees came to the Tule River, the old-time bird and animal people had no fire. Tro'-khud, the Eagle, spoke to his son, Lim'-ik, the Prairie Falcon. He said, "I see a light over to the west. Wi'-ness, the First Man, lives there. He has some fire, which makes light. Call all of the people together. We will go over and get some of the fire."

Lim'-ik told all of the people, and they went across the wide valley and a great lake. They crossed the hills and plains. In a valley far to the west they found Wi'-ness and his fire.[1] He was guarding the fire closely.

Eagle asked Wi'-ness for some fire, but he refused. Then all of the old-time bird and animal people tried to take some of the fire. Wah'-cut, the Heron tried. He could reach a long distance, but he could not get the fire. Wee-hay'-sit, the Mountain Lion, tried. So did No-ho'-o, the Grizzly Bear, and Haw-tun'-ut, the Gopher Snake, but Wi'-ness kept all of them from obtaining any fire.

After everyone else had tried, Oon'-cut, the Gopher, said, "Let me try. I can get some of that fire." All of the old-time people sat down around the fire to see what Oon'-cut would do. He dug a hole behind them, where Wi'-ness could not see him. Then he went under the ground to where the fire was burning. He dug to the surface of the ground. He peeked out. Wi'-ness was not looking.

Oon'-cut hurriedly took some of the fire in his paws and stuffed it into the pockets of his cheeks. Wi'-ness saw him do that, but Oon'-cut backed into the hole so quickly that Wi'-ness could not stop him. Digging underground toward the east, Oon'-cut started back to the old village on the Tule River.[2]

"After everyone had tried, Oon'-cut, the Gopher, said, 'Let me try. I can get some of that fire.'" —Courtesy Susafri, Red Princess Productions, istockphotos

He went under the plains and hills, deep under the great lake, toward the Sierra Nevada.[3] When he was almost there, Oon'-cut thought," I guess Wi'-ness will not see me now, so I can come up safely."

When Oon'-cut came to the surface, it was night. Wi'-ness could see the light of the fire that Oon'-cut was carrying. He ran after Oon'-cut as fast as he could. He almost caught him. But Oon'-cut went under the ground again and did not come up until he arrived at the village.

So Oon'-cut, the Gopher, obtained the first fire for the old-time bird and animal people. They kept his fire and gave it to the Yauh'-dahn-chee Indians at their old beginning village of Chuh-muk'-tow.

—Adapted from Frank F. Latta, *California Indian Folklore.*[4]

THE SIZE OF THE YOKUTS TERRITORY WAS EXTENSIVE. It covered over three hundred square miles, stretching from the Stockton Delta to the Tehachapi Mountains, and from the western foothills of the Sierra Nevada across the San Joaquin Valley plains to the Coast Ranges. Within the Yokuts' forty to sixty tribal divisions were hundreds of communities comprising an estimated twenty thousand to forty thousand people living in a mostly friendly relationship with one another.

"They were a tall, well built people," ethnographer A. L. Kroeber wrote of them, "of open outlook, frank, upstanding, casual and unceremonious, optimistic and friendly, fond of laughter, not given to cares of property or too much worry about tomorrow; and they lived in direct simple relation to their land and the world, to its animals, spirits and gods, and to one another."[5]

Descended from Penutian immigrants, the Yokuts called themselves Yokoch, or "peoples." They remained one linguistic and cultural family with only small variations in dialect, and they have been described as the only true related group of tribes of California, with a distinct name and a common language and territory.

The foothill Yokuts of the central and southern Sierra were the most populous tribes of the Yokuts nation. They flourished in every major river drainage from the south bank of the Fresno River to the Kern, with permanent villages nestled on bluffs and riverbanks at elevations between 1,500 and 4,000 feet.

According to Wukchumni Yokuts legend, after the Eagle, Lion, Wolf, and Coyote created

The foothill Yokuts erected conical tule-reed dwellings rather than the dome-shaped structures of the valley Yokuts and the Tubatulabal. —Illustration by Jana Botkin, Cabin Arts, adapted from A. H. Gayton, *Yokuts and Western Mono Ethnography*

human beings, the new people congregated near a sweathouse in the mountains rising above the southern end of California's Central Valley. They lived and multiplied there until they became so numerous they were threatened with starvation.

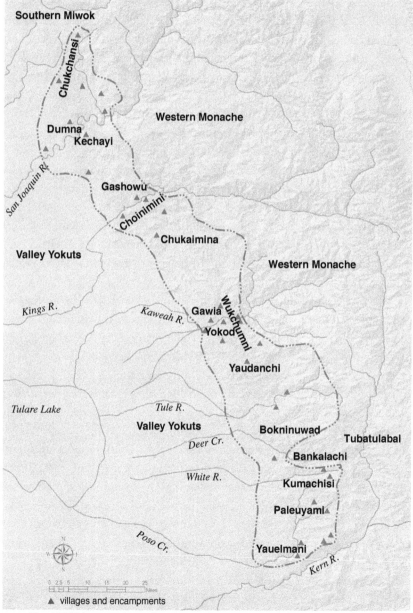

Foothill Yokuts territory showing major groups and their main villages
—Adapted from A. H. Gayton, *Yokuts and Western Mono Ethnography*, and A. L. Kroeber, *Handbook of the Indians of California*

Tro'-khud, the Eagle, knew he must distribute these people over more of the world, so he took them on a great pilgrimage. He settled the Yauelmani along the lower Kern River and an area south of it; the Paleuyami, north of the Kern and on Poso Creek; the Kumachisi and Shoshonean Tubatulabal and Bankalachi, on White River and upper Deer Creek; the Bokninuwad and Yaudanchi, on the Tule River and lower Deer Creek; the Yokod, on Yokohl Creek and across to the Kaweah. The Wukchumni and Gawia lived on the Kaweah River, above where it ran into the great Central Valley. The Chukaimina and the Choinimini settled in the foothills of the Kings River. The Gashowu, Kechayi, and Dumna were on the San Joaquin River. The Chukchansi lived in the foothills along the south side of the Fresno River, across from the Miwok Pohonichi, who lived on the north side.

As diverse and scattered as these individual tribes were, the foothill Yokuts had much in common. They were generally a peaceful people, for they all had abundant resources at their disposal. Their environment had several species of oaks; numerous varieties of grasses, clovers, and seeds; waterfowl that wintered in the Central Valley on the immense Tulare, Buena Vista, and Kern lakes; countless small animals, birds, and edible insects; tule elk in herds of thousands in the lowlands; deer and bear in the mountains and foothills; and fish in virtually every stream.

This fertile environment allowed the Yokuts a standard of living that was exceptional among prehistoric peoples in North America, giving them time to create permanent communities that provided many social advantages. Some of their daily jobs were specialized. They developed separate work sites for the manufacture of implements and for food processing. A complex language with an involved system of verb and noun stem-shapes emerged. An intricate economic system regulated trade and money exchanges, and they had policies for dealings with other tribes.

The Yokuts had a highly structured society with strict taboos and traditions. Yokuts social structure was based on patriarchal hierarchies and lines of descent with moieties—dual-structured societies—from the Kings River area north. There was a set protocol for every activity and situation. The reciprocation of gifts, the cooperative sharing of hunting and gathering territories, and the arts of compromise and mediation were Yokuts traditions. "A man must be mediocre, or depart only a little way from the norm in order to be a success," one Yaudanchi Yokuts reported. "A man who was too generous and held open house with plenty of food too often would incite the jealousy of the chief."[6]

Even though Yokuts had strict rules and expectations, they had the time and freedom to develop individual skills and talents, too. Some of the most beautiful basketry work in the world was woven by the Yokuts. Duck decoys looked so true-to-life that when the first Caucasian hunters saw them, they shot them, thinking they were real. Poetry through songs evolved, and story-telling flourished. Pictographs, costuming, and body painting reflected artistic expression.

Because nature provided them with so much, the Yokuts' relationship to the natural world ran deep. In 1977, historian Frank F. Latta wrote of this relationship, based on his conversations with Yokuts elders:

> These river people were at home beside broad, quiet streams beneath oak trees which often towered one hundred fifty feet in the air, and among the branches of which raven, crow, woodpecker, blue jay, wood duck, magpie and dozens of other birds constantly were clamoring. Lashed to their cradle boards, among the first words learned by Yokuts children were the Yokuts names for these birds, and the first natural history and folklore taught to them concerned those same birds; how Pah-dah-dut, the woodpecker, received his name from the sound of his hammering; how the blue jay planted the oak trees; how, in a game of shinny, the wood duck obtained his colors from all creatures of the forest; how the magpie taught the newly created Indians to talk.[7]

Cultural traditions were often based on natural connections as well. Traditions of family and lineage had been handed down through countless generations from the original animal people. Everything was guided by male succession, with each child following the name and totem of the father. Each family adhered to the responsibilities of its totem animal. The Eagle line gave birth to chiefs; the Dove, to winatum messengers; the Cougar, to assistant chiefs; the Raven, to dance leaders; the Magpie, to spokesmen or criers; and the Coyote, to clowns. Shamans, however, were not born into their position, but were called by the rattlesnake, bear, or water animals to practice their supernatural powers.

It was essential to follow careful protocol to show respect for one's totemic animal. No animal could be killed or eaten by its totemic family. If a person outside the family killed and ate the animal, the person must give the family a payment as redemption and to honor the animal. If an animal was captured or made a pet, a member of the totemic family usually bought it to keep or set free.

There were also animal dream helpers outside the totemic structure. These magic animals offered special powers to the dreamer. Dreaming of an eagle could make one rich. A falcon could help a person keep crowds quiet. A cougar brought strength and hunting success.

Shamans had special dream helpers, including the coyote, the weasel, and the skunk. The owl, who helped the huhuna dancer, was also a favorite of shamans, for owls could see anything. The antelope could help a man become a shaman or a doctor, and anyone who took this dream helper might become rich, but at a cost. To follow the antelope required adhering to many rules, and this animal's followers did not live long lives.

The pronghorn antelope, a very important food source for the foothill Yokuts, had important spiritual powers, especially for shamans. —Courtesy Elemental Imaging, stockphotos

IN THE YOKUTS LANGUAGE, there were no words for right and wrong. There were only good actions and bad, with moral conduct expressed through the medium of good manners. Social customs guided those manners: the avoidance of too much contact between in-laws; the use of kinship terms to show respect; showing respect for elders at all times; restraining anger and jealousy; asking permission in any activity that involved others; and always speaking with politeness and projecting a demeanor of affability. It was also important

Family meals were carefully guarded, and the food had to be eaten as soon as it was prepared. —Courtesy F. Latta and A. Barr, from Kern River historical reenactment, Tulare County Office of Education

to avoid the places where individuals prayed and contemplated, especially the cache and meditation places of shamans.

The health of both individuals and the social order required discipline and the firm observance of taboos. Cramp-inducing tobacco and lime emetics were often drunk to cleanse the stomach. Women abstained from meat and grease during menses and pregnancy. Any newborns with deformities—caused by witchcraft or an evil shaman—were destroyed. Women and children had to stay away from the sweathouses, which only the men were privileged to use.

Special precautions were taken against evildoing shamans. One had to take care not to leave hair, saliva, or discarded clothing available to shamans who might use them to create sickness or death. All food was prepared cautiously and not allowed to sit uneaten, so malicious shamans could not poison it.

After a death, the protocols for the surviving family members were of great importance: restraint from washing one's face; singeing the hair short; avoiding public gatherings; abstinence from meat; refraining from speaking of the dead; changing the name of anyone named after the deceased; honoring the cremation of those who had died away from home, had met a violent death, or wished not to be buried; respecting the role of the beardaches, or transvestites, as undertakers and paying them at the annual mourning ceremony.

Feasts and ceremonies were held often. The greatest gathering of all was the annual autumn mourning ceremony, which lasted six days and nights. The event was held to absolve mourning families of their bereavement duties and to celebrate kinship and intertribal ties. There were also ceremonies and dances held purely for pleasure. The kam dance was a social dance performed by both men and women, often in all-night sessions, accompanied by gambling games. In the male huhuna dance, money was hidden and searched for. The watiyod dance was performed by shamans for the entertainment of the villagers.

Special ceremonies and rituals were held for boys and girls reaching puberty. These rites of passage helped instill and preserve community traditions and values. Late-night winter swims were required of all adolescents to make them strong, healthy, self-disciplined, and accepting of life's hardships. Elders insisted all young people participate in rough-house dances on moonlit summer nights to overcome shyness. Clowns performed ribald acts at most celebrations so there would be no secrets or misconceptions about sex and human nature.

The jimsonweed ritual was not compulsory, but adolescents were encouraged to endure it to insure future good health and a long life. It was believed the frightening visions brought on by the datura mixture helped a young person understand the supernatural world; they also might bring the participant a dream helper. The adolescent's family and friends participated in the ceremony and showed him or her their support. The young person's whole family committed to a three-month sexual abstinence before and after the ceremony and gave the initiate special care and attention. Observing these traditions served to bond the adolescent to his or her community.

TO MANAGE SUCH A WIDESPREAD PEOPLE, strong leadership was essential. Yokuts chiefs, called tiyas, were known for their skills in governance. Although sometimes a good chief would bribe a doctor to kill some man he thought ought to be killed, traditionally, the tiya of each Yokuts tribe maintained a reputation for being generous, honest, caring, and fair.

Most tiyas were of the Eagle totem family lineage, although some bands occasionally appointed one who was not. There were a few women who became sub-chiefs, but only in cases where there were no suitable males in the Eagle line. It would be difficult for those outside the Eagle family to succeed, for the tiya's duties, traditions, and rules of protocol and demeanor were varied and complex, hard to fully understand without the strict training from childhood that only patrilineal succession can provide.

A tiya was usually in charge of all the villages along a particular river drainage, and his responsibilities were diverse. He had to make certain he could provide for his own family adequately so they all could perform their defined duties as participants in the title of tiya. He was expected to settle quarrels of all kinds: to pacify competing shamans so they would

A Yokuts chief—Courtesy F. Latta and A. Barr, from Kern River historical reenactment, Tulare County Office of Education

not practice evil medicine on each other; to mediate village and intertribal disputes over gathering and hunting grounds, granary rights, and fish catch distributions; and even to settle squabbles in games and contests.

Protecting Yokuts territory and individual villages required the chief's constant attention. Intertribal raids were not uncommon, instigated in retaliation for another group's incursion into hunting or gathering grounds, a murder, an attack on a woman, or the sorcery of a shaman. Even though potential warriors were plentiful, the battles were usually small, often fought from the cover of rocks and trees. After any altercation, the chiefs or village sub-chiefs of the combatants would meet to work out a peace agreement, and afterward they often sponsored a feast for both sides.

Another major job for the tiya was to determine the schedule for each family's annual gathering and hunting trips, rotating the best spots to alleviate competition. All communal decisions were the tiya's: the times and places of cooperative hunts, fishing forays, and trading expeditions; when to build a new communal sweathouse; where additional houses could be built; whether the house of someone who had died should be occupied by another family or torn down.

The tiya was also responsible for maintaining an efficient courier system of winatums, who carried messages between Yokuts villages and into neighboring tribal territories. He assigned men to maintain signal fires on outlying hills to announce the approach of strangers and natural disasters such as floods and wildfires. He was also expected to guide his people through social disasters, such as the havoc caused when a shaman became evil and killed someone.

When an important decision had to be made, the tiya often held council with other tiyas, his village sub-chiefs, and respected elders. They might discuss the issue of whether a malpracticing shaman must be killed, a nonconforming member of one of the villages should be banished, or a battle should be waged against a neighboring tribe. But most often, his councils concerned plans for the most important function of the year—the annual mourning ceremony.

ON THE KAWEAH RIVER, the Wukchumni chief often sat in council with his sub-chiefs from surrounding villages. There was one from the hamlet of Pahdin, the place where an evil spirit sometimes pulled swimmers under the water to drown. Others were from Gotau, a hamlet higher on the river; from Choyo, a hillside village with a fine spring; and from Ustunu, over the southeast hills above the Yokohl Valley. Even if no others could come, he could always count on the chief from Gutsnumi, a village not far from the main village of Daiapnusa, and also the chief from Hoganu, on Lime Kiln Creek, the last village between the foothills and the plains.

Each year, these sub-chiefs came to Daiapnusa to confer about the money needed for the annual mourning ceremony. If several families had experienced death, more money would be needed; some families had no wealth, and the head chief was responsible for their debts. He often had to pay for the first mourning and burial with no promise that the family could ever repay him. He was also required to lend the families money for their part in the mourning ceremony.

All year long, villagers requested money from the tiya. Deaths or illness in a family, poor hunting or gathering seasons, drought, insect invasions, other misfortunes brought on by malevolent shamans—all had to be handled by the

A foothill river at flood stage. The southern Sierra Yokuts experienced many floods, as the area's steep waterways flowed unchecked during heavy rains. —Courtesy Three Rivers Museum archives

tiya. At times, great floods would come down the rivers, destroying homes and granaries, and the tiya was responsible for his people's shelter, feeding, and care until new homes could be constructed. If floods wreaked havoc in the plains below, the villages of the lower Kaweah Delta streams and Tulare Lake sometimes would completely lose their lands. Then, the winatums, or messengers, of other other chiefs would come up the river to the Wukchumnis asking for loans.

The tiya had many other expenses. He had to pay his own winatum each time he had a message to send; the performers of all the year's celebrations; the bear and rattlesnake shamans for their rituals to bring a good acorn harvest and to protect his people from snakebites. When a weather shaman visited, the tiya often paid twice, first to bring the rain, then to shut it off if it became a raging torrent.

The tiya had to honor the tradition of providing housing, meals, and entertainment for all guests, including those from other Yokuts hamlets and from different California tribes. He also had to support his own large family, which often included two wives, as well as their widowed mothers and his own, and any of the family's unmarried children. It was also essential that the tiya make or purchase the finest hunting and fishing equipment for his sons, as befitted those of the Eagle lineage.

Wives, sisters, and daughters of his family were also termed tiya, with an important role as ceremonial hostesses. These women were expected to be ready at any moment to serve food to visitors, and they were responsible for preparing and serving large quantities of food at ceremonial functions.

It was difficult to keep up with the demands for money and services, so before each year's mourning ceremony, the tiya would call his sub-chiefs together to work out the finances. First they counted all the current resources from their combined treasuries, figuring their worth in lengths of strung money. Some of these were shells procured from trade with the Chumash tribes on the coast. Others were steatite beads mined and fashioned by the Yokodo people near present-day Lindsay. Money made from the Pismo clam and steatite had the highest value, and chawik, made from little periwinkle or olivella shells, the least.

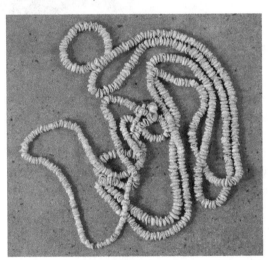

Strands of steatite (soapstone) beads. Used as money, locally mined steatite was of the highest value. —Courtesy Tulare County Museum

Next, they estimated the monies that would be coming in from the mourning ceremony. That would include payments from the mourning hosts, minus the costs of the singers, dancers, shamans, and winatums. The chief's family would also receive food and other gifts, some of which they might trade for money.

The most important item on the balance sheet was the interest that could be collected at the mourning ceremony for all the loans the tiya and his sub-chiefs had made during the year—often at 50 percent and sometimes even

Yokuts baskets, valued for their quality and beauty, were important trade items among all tribes.
—Courtesy Tulare County Museum

100 percent rates. If these assets still fell short of their needs, the tiya's family could sell gifts they had received from other tribes: fine obsidian arrowheads and tools from the Owens Valley; sinew-backed mountain cedar hunting bows; salt from the coastal Chumash and eastern desert Monache; and carved steatite bowls.

There were other possible ways to raise revenue as well. The council members could increase the amount of payment required of the mourning hosts. They could demand payment from the four temporary sub-chiefs, called tuye'i, whose only job was to help manage the annual mourning ceremony and help pay for any deficits that might accrue. The tuye'i came from families of some wealth and were obligated to help. But the chiefs hesitated to burden them further, for these families often made loans of their own.

If the deficit was serious, the tiya might have to ask his people to create more items for trade or sale. Hunting parties could procure animal skins and meat; the men could make arrowheads from obsidian preforms; the women could create baskets, rabbit-skin blankets, and deerskin skirts and grind acorn meal. The council might also send out performers to entertain other tribes and take a portion of the money they made. And if all that wasn't enough, the chiefs could send their winatums to neighboring tribes to ask for donations of trading items to be reciprocated in a greater amount sometime after the ceremonies, or even to ask for cash loans.

AFTER MONTHS OF PLANNING AND PREPARATIONS, the annual mourning ceremony would take place outside the village of Daiapnusa. People from all over the Central Valley and foothills attended, gathering in the hundreds to enjoy dances, games, feasts, gambling, trading, and socializing. The bonds between the Wukchumni and their reciprocal tribe, the Tule River Yaudanchi, would be strengthened, and new alliances were often forged. Several inter-tribal marriages might be arranged, which would help foster trade and mutual resource management.

To a large extent, the success of the mourning ceremony helped assure the tiya's reputation as a great chief. It was an image a tiya worked hard to achieve, so that his memory would be honored for at least four generations, and his name might be carried on to future Eagle chiefs, in alternate genera-tions, as long as the Yokuts people survived.

8. The Western Monache

THE MONACHE COME TO THE SIERRA NEVADA
A Nim Western Monache Tale

The Nim heard the sound of water hitting a shoreline. They kept hearing the sound for days. They wondered what it was, so they sent people to see. The people got to a place and saw a wall of water coming toward them. They hurried back to the rest of the people and said, "There is water coming. It will be here in a week."

"The water kept coming and the people went higher and higher into the mountains. They reached the highest mountain." Many prehistoric tales told of great waters flooding the lowlands. —Courtesy Sequoia National Park archives

All the people started preparing food to take with them to the high country. They pounded acorn, berries, and seeds. They packed dry meat and took off for higher ground. Some people stayed to watch and send messages back to the others.

The water kept coming and the people went higher and higher into the mountains. They reached the highest mountain. There they lived with the animals. They lived together for weeks and weeks. The water receded and the Nim followed it back to their homes.

—Adapted from Gaylen D. Lee,

Walking Where We Lived: Memoirs of a Mono Indian Family.[1]

THE WESTERN MONACHE (or Western Mono)[2] migrated during a cool, moist period in the Sierra Nevada at the onset of the Little Ice Age. Separating from other Paiute peoples, they moved from the east side of the Sierra Nevada to the west side 400 to 700 years ago (around AD 1300 to 1600). What caused their migration from the Mono Lake and Owens Valley region into the Fresno, San Joaquin, Kings, Kaweah, and upper Tule river drainages is a mystery. Descendants of the Great Basin Numic-speaking peoples, they crossed to the west side of the Sierra crest to settle between the 3,000- to 7,000-foot elevations, above the villages of the Penutian-speaking Yokuts tribes. It was a resource-rich area, ranging from oak woodland and grasslands, where native bunchgrasses provided seed and animal grazing grounds, into forests of black oak, ponderosa pine, cedar, white fir, sugar pine, and some sequoia groves.

Long before the Monache arrived, this had been the traditional summer hunting and gathering grounds of the foothill Yokuts. In the Kings River drainage on Dinkey Creek, projectile points indicate that there were fairly large, multiple occupations at the 5,700- to 5,800-foot elevation as early as 3,000 to 6,000 years ago.

To have foreign-speaking people invade and claim a long-established Yokuts territory could have created major battles. But evidence to date shows nothing to indicate that such was the case. Although several small territorial clashes may have occurred, it seems to have been a fairly friendly infiltration.

Monache territory, such as the Siberian Outpost, held some of the highest summer occupation and hunting areas in the Sierra Nevada. —Courtesy Tom Burge, Sequoia National Park archives

One Yokuts story tells of frays between the Waksachi Monache and their Yokuts neighbors near Eshom Valley, until one Yokuts chief proposed a conference between the leaders of the two groups. A treaty of peace was agreed upon, and a great feast followed. From then on, tribal disturbances were small, local, and infrequent.[3]

There could have been several reasons for the general lack of hostility. The Monache migration may have taken place over a long period of time, so their influx at any one time may have been so small as to be acceptable to most Yokuts people. Also, because the occupation came during a relatively moist period, the control of resources may not have been a large issue. Artifacts and traditions speak of joint use of hunting and foraging lands above present Three Rivers by the Wukchumni Yokuts and the Waksachi and Potwisha Monache tribes. The North Fork Mono and eastern Long Valley Paiutes also shared trading and hunting grounds.

As the Monache and Yokuts interacted and intermarried, their two cultures began to blend, but with several variations. Some Western Monache families practiced the Yokuts customs of moieties, but did not always follow the totemic rituals or patrilineal traditions. Moiety chiefs had no governmental power, but acted solely as ceremonial figures. The male head of a household was each family's authority figure.

The Western Monache were a self-sufficient people with a culture that functioned in an often harsh environment. They lived in small, mobile community units that could move quickly and easily. Unlike the large, settled Yokuts, the Monache were loosely organized, without central governmental and social traditions. The villages were merely extended family groups that moved from one seasonally preferred occupation site to another within the loosely defined boundaries of Western Monache lands. "Each individual in the course of a normal life-time lived in many hamlets and camps," Edward Gifford found in his studies. "Even the largest hamlet was ephemeral, and in

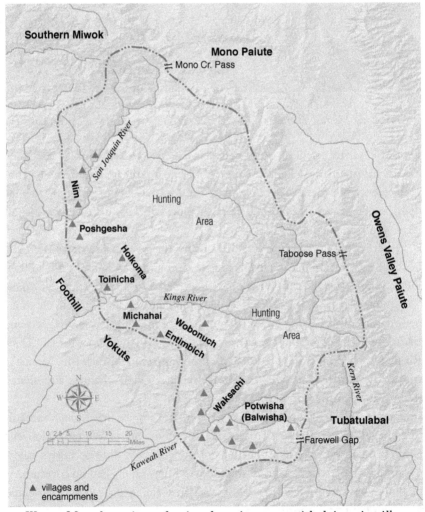

Western Monache territory, showing the major groups with their main village sites —Adapted from A. H. Gayton, *Yokuts and Western Mono Ethnography,* and A. L. Kroeber, *Handbook of the Indians of California*

a few seasons the households comprising it were living elsewhere, often in association with new neighbors."[4]

The entire Western Monache population numbered only eighteen hundred to two thousand in precontact times. As many as twelve different tribal subgroups, each with its own headman, claimed territories from the Fresno River drainage south to the Kaweah drainage and upper Tule River. These subgroups were the Nim (which included the North Fork,) Poshgesha, Kwetah, Kokoheba, Toinicha, Holkoma (or Tuhukwaj), Wobonuch, Entimbich, Michahai, Waksachi, and Potwisha.

The principal villages below the 4,000-foot snow line were mostly winter camps. Elevations between 7,000 and 8,000 feet held many summer occupation sites. These were evidently visited year after year by several families sharing the high mountain resources. Hunting camps, plant-gathering bases, and trading stations proliferated. Trails that snaked between foothill villages eventually led to every possible pass. Those crossing into or out of Paiute territory to gather, hunt, trade, or visit made high camps all along the trails. A trip by the North Fork Monache to the Owens Valley area could entail nine or ten days of travel, with frequent stops at creeks, springs, and meadows for hunting and food preparation.

Only because the native populations remained fairly small and transient was the High Sierra environment able to sustain adequate food and water resources for these Western Monache communities.

ALL WESTERN MONACHE MEN WERE HUNTERS. They usually worked in small groups, all following prescribed protocols for a successful hunt. The hunters fasted for at least a day before the hunt, in order to eliminate any food smells. To rid their bodies of human smells, they spent hours in a sweat lodge and bathed afterwards. The night before the hunt, they slept inside a shelter so the deer wouldn't see their shadows against the rising moon.

The manufacture of dependable hunting equipment occupied much of the men's time. They crafted bows, arrows, quivers, and spring traps according to specifications handed down from generation to generation. Self, or plain, bows were made for daily family use from California laurel or elderwood, while long, sinew-backed, recurved bows made from the sapwood of mountain cedar were highly valued as trading items.

Making the recurved bows was an intricate process. First, the wood was heated over glowing coals, then curved over one knee and bent slowly, carefully, bit by bit, over a period of three to six days until it held a perfect shape. Then it was honed with flint for a few more days and finally massaged with deer's marrow to polish and add elasticity to the wood. The bowstring was made from unbroken sinew pulled from the long back muscles of a deer, split with flint into small fibers, and fastened onto the flat back of the bow with glue made of liquid from boiled deer brains or animal joints mixed with pitch.

The Western Monache made several types of arrows from different wood. Small bird arrows were made from alder, small game arrows from willow, and deer arrows from cane and oak sprouts. They attached squirrel-hawk wing feathers to each arrow so it would fly straight and true. Most arrowheads were carved from obsidian preforms that they gathered from the Fish Springs area of the Owens Valley or acquired in trade with the Owens Valley Paiute and Eastern Mammoth area Monache. Their quivers were made out of deer or antelope hides, or of fox skins with the fur left on.

The methods of a hunt were designed to be efficient and effective. Western Monache hunters often poisoned their arrows with rotted deer liver and rattlesnake venom in order to assure a kill. They set the nooses of spring traps

A typical Sierra hunter's regalia. While the Monache used the self, or plain, bow (shown here) for daily use, they were noted for their shorter recurved bows, which were carefully crafted with upward curves at the ends, making them easier to manage than other bows. —Courtesy F. Latta and A. Barr, from Kern River historical reenactment, Tulare County Office of Education

to guarantee an instant death. They made horned deer- and antelope-head disguises to try to trick the animals they stalked. Sometimes they joined other hunters from as far away as the eastern deserts, setting encircling fires to drive the deer into ambush. They learned from the neighboring Shoshones how to run bighorn sheep for miles in the summer heat until their hooves peeled off, disabling them for the kill.

In some cases the Monache may have been too successful in their pursuit of game. In several areas of the Sierra, the bighorn sheep and pronghorn antelope were overhunted long before the arrival of Euro-Americans. Accounts from the Owens Valley area tell of hunting cults that depleted the bighorn sheep in both the Sierra and Coso ranges. Antelope drives in the Owens Valley and San Joaquin Valley foothills were so effective that the herds sometimes had to be allowed to recover for ten or fifteen years before another drive was held.

Unlike the Yokuts, the Western Monache never apologized to an animal for killing it. Young men often went on hunting ventures just for practice, and sometimes they hunted the grizzly bear for sport. Grizzly hunting was unusual among Sierra tribes, as most considered the grizzly bear a link between humans and animals and possibly even humans themselves. The hunters delighted in sharing their tales of conquest, with the best stories coming from men of the Cougar totem, for they had special hunting powers.

Western Monache men were also traders, and the women often joined them on trading excursions. Most of the time, trading parties stayed close to home, meeting near their hunting boundaries. But each year, a few small

Bighorn sheep roamed ch of the High Sierra rehistoric times. They were heavily hunted.
—Courtesy Nature's Display, R & R Visions, istockphotos

groups of men and women embarked on summer expeditions to the Paiute and Tubatulabal territories. One major trading encampment lay at the confluence of the Little Kern and North Fork Kern, in the Round and Trout Meadows area. There, the Western Monache would meet with the Tubatulabal, Tule River Yokuts, and Owens Valley Paiute, engaging in days-long bargaining sessions. The multilingual Western Monache could speak dialects of both the Penutian and Numic languages, so they acted as the middlemen in such negotiations.

Western Monache traders also set up shop all along the western trade routes, where they bartered with the foothill Yokuts, offering their prized sinew-backed bows, clay pottery, black paint, black sword-fern root, and redbud bark. In exchange, they received tule elk skins, soaproot brushes, grass salt, baskets, tule mats, roots, bunchgrass seeds, and herbs. With easterners,

Mono Pass was a major trade route between the Western Monache and Mono Lake Paiute. —Photo by G. K. Gilbert (1908), courtesy USGS Photographic Library

they bargained not only with their sinew-backed bows, but also acorns, gray-pine and sugar-pine nuts, manzanita berries, sow berries from the squawbush, deer and antelope skins, steatite, and willow baskets. In return, they received prized obsidian blanks and arrowheads, woven water bottles sealed with pitch, fox-skin leggings, and rabbit-skin blankets. They also made a profit reselling items such as Yokuts asphaltum and coastal Chumash shell money to the eastern tribes, and reselling the easterners' piñon nuts, water bottles, rock salt, and paints to the Yokuts.

A trading expedition was always a time of excitement, a chance to meet men, women, boys, and girls of different tribes. It was in the trading camps that the blending of cultures took place, for while the distances traveled by each group were relatively short, the goods exchanged had often been passed over hundreds of miles. Some hunters met their future wives in these trading

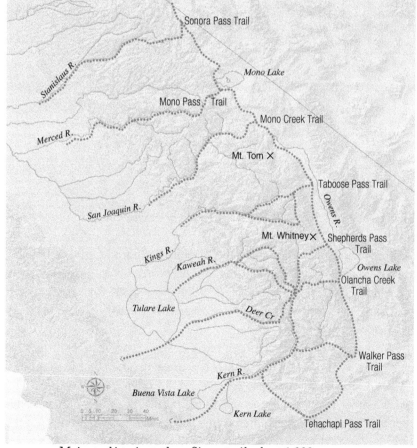

Major prehistoric southern Sierra trails about 1,000 years ago.

camps. Occasionally, a young Paiute woman from the Owens Valley or Mono Lake area might decide to follow a young Western Monache man home to his village and end up marrying him. Sometimes a whole family would visit a trading partner's village and stay for months or even years. Marriages between Western Monache and Yokuts were common.

Trade depended on a system of good trails. Young Monache men often scouted new trails looking for faster and better routes to Paiute, Tubatulabal, and Yokuts villages. In wooded country, trails might trace a stream; in open areas, they often climbed to the ridges, where there were fewer shrubs to hinder travel or to hide enemies or evil spirits. Forest trails often followed animal paths, especially those of bears, for they were deeply etched and easy to follow. Almost always, the backcountry trails took the most direct route possible, even if the terrain was difficult, since they were used by strong young men and women who could climb steep peaks and ridges. Only the lower trails leading to summer villages needed to be easier for the older people and little children.

There were several trading trails that the Monache used to cross the Sierra. For example, one ran up the South Fork of the Kings River to Taboose Pass. To the north, on the Middle Fork of the Kings, a trail left the acorn grounds at Simpson Meadows and followed Dougherty Creek, crossing the Cirque Crest to join the South Fork trail. There were also several trans-Sierra routes that ran east from the Kaweah and Kern river drainages to Owens Lake. Some trails circled large territories of the western slopes without crossing the Sierra crest.

GROWING UP FOR A MONACHE BOY was little else but learning. He spent years learning the methods and protocols of hunting and how to make weapons. He studied the routes and distances of both hunting and trading trails. His elders taught him all the dialects of neighboring tribes and ways to negotiate with them. As he learned how to provide for himself and for the family he would eventually have, there was almost no time for games and leisure pursuits.

Living in a small family grouping that moved often, a youth had little contact with boys and girls his own age other than family members. Even if there was another camp close by, he would often be off with his father and the other men on hunting and trading expeditions. The only prolonged opportunity he had to meet other young people was when his family left their summer camps to spend the winter at a lower foothill village. There he would be in close proximity to several hamlets that would meet for special occasions. Often, the fall dances, games, and ceremonies were the only chance a boy had to socialize with peers who lived outside his family's village.

Just as important as his ties to others was a boy's tie to the natural world. Western Monache tradition was to honor all animals, and young people were steeped in the myths of prehuman time, when animals behaved like people. He understood the connectedness of the world and that animals, birds, and humans were all equally important.

The plant kingdom, too, held lessons. One father showed his son a lodgepole pine that had grown straight and strong since its youth. Then he showed the boy a tree that had no shape, but was all legs and arms reaching out in different directions. The old, straight, one-trunked lodgepole had led a sheltered life like the Yokuts, the boy's father told his son. But the Western Monache always had many trunks and branches bent and twisted by the winds and the seasons of the mountains. Like the lodgepole pines on high peaks, they had to be many shapes if they were to survive.[5]

From the time he was a baby, a boy's father, mother, and older relatives tutored him to respect the natural forces that surrounded him and to work with them rather than trying to overcome them. His elders told him stories explaining all natural phenomena. The phases of the moon, eclipses of the

A bent pine in what was once Monache territory
—Courtesy Laurel DiSilvestro

sun, shooting stars, thunder and lightning—all were part of the world and nothing to fear.

He learned, too, what should be feared. When streams were rushing with spring runoff, he must walk a few extra miles to reach a safe crossing. If there was an earthquake, he should watch for falling rock. When a winter storm came early to the highlands, he should abandon the tempting warmth and comfort of his cedar-bark hunting shelter lest he become trapped in deep snows.

The Western Monache encouraged more self-sufficiency than most California native groups, but it was necessary for survival in the wilderness. Still, there were traditions, rules, taboos, and social restrictions that had to be followed. Early each morning, a boy would rise to talk with the spirit of the dawn about any dreams he had had. If they were good dreams, he would ask the dawn to make them true, and if they were bad, he would tell the sun to chase them away. Sometimes he would have dreams of the animal spirits that could guide him in his daily pursuits. If his hunting skills were not yet fully developed, perhaps it was because he had not yet dreamed of the cougar. Or, perhaps, the elders would tell him, it was because of a lack of patience.

Patience was not simply a virtue; it was life itself. It was waiting for antelope and deer to appear, for fish to run in the spring, for the life-giving

winter rains and the warmth of the summer sun. It was accepting the ideas of other men as they were building a fishing weir. It was sitting quietly for hours, listening to sounds from miles around and watching all the small movements of the life surrounding him. It was learning how to tolerate cold mountain mornings without extra clothing, adapting one's eyesight to the darkness of a moonless night, and relaxing through the heat of an August day.

Rock falls are common throughout the High Sierra region. They are often generated by melting ice adhesions or earthquakes. —From author's files

A young Monache boy also learned pride—in his people, his family, and his own strengths and skills. If he was not as great a hunter as some, he might have other talents that his people honored and respected. He might become known for the fine hunting implements he created, or for his carving abilities in making flutes of elderwood and cane, oak wood storage vessels, beautiful soapstone tobacco pipes, or bowls carved out of steatite to supplement the utilitarian clay models made by the women and girls.

He learned respect for others, including those of different tribes, even when there were conflicts. When a group of Mono Lake Paiute crossed over the Mammoth Crest and passed the boundary of Western Monache territory to use their hunting grounds without permission, his elders cautioned it was best to parley with them rather than attack. Even war demanded honor and respect. He and the other hunters formed shorter bows to be used in close battle and made slings that would deter but seldom kill. They also fashioned arrows with the obsidian firmly lashed to the foreshaft so they could be pulled out of a person's body.

In his wanderings, a boy would discover signs of the ancient people, who were a mystery to all. He would see discarded metates, the flat grinding stones that women no longer used. He might find an old atlatl, the spear-throwing device that bows and arrows had long since replaced. He might come near sequoia groves in the drainages of the Fresno, Kaweah, and Tule rivers, where huge basins seemed to have been ground out of the granite bedrock. Old storytellers said they were the mortars of ancient giants whose size matched that of *Toos-pung'-ish*, the sacred sequoia.[6]

When the boy became a man, he would start his own family. Although cohabitation was not frowned upon, almost all Western Monache men married. The choice of a bride was his own

Large granite bedrock basins dot the Southern Sierra. Their purpose has been widely debated.
—Courtesy Sequoia National Park archives

as long as she wasn't of his own bloodline. Cross-cousin marriage was taboo. If he chose a woman who had already lived in several households, whether in connubial relationships or not, there was no bride price to be paid. But if he chose a girl who had always lived with her parents, he would have to pay for her with shell money or trade items. Payment was made to the girl's father, or to her mother if the father had died.

If the young man was the oldest son in a family, he and his wife would often live with her parents for six to eighteen months, then move to his father's household. If he was a younger son, he would construct homes close to his parents at the various settlements they used during a year. The members of his immediate family could include his mother-in-law as well as his own unmarried sisters and brothers.

As a man grew older, his wife might die or run away, and he would take a new bride. Some men took second wives if their first one proved to be barren; others divorced them. Divorce could also result if a woman did not accept a second wife, or if she was slothful or talked too much. Divorce simply meant a woman or man left the family compound, taking his or her personal possessions with them.

Most family units stayed intact and maintained close relationships with each other. A man would take an active part in his family's life. Like his own father, he would spend his years roaming the Sierra, now with his own boys to teach, and he might tell each of them the story of the lodgepole pine. By then, the winds and the seasons would have bent and twisted him into his own individual Monache shape. Finally he would die and be cremated, and his ashes would blow over the mountains that had always been his home.

9. The Sierra Miwok

THE SEARCH FOR THE DEER
A Central Sierra Miwok Tale

"What is the matter? What is the trouble that we see no deer? Have any of you seen their tracks?" the people asked. "What shall we eat, if we do not find the deer?"

The hunters went into the hills toward the north and searched daily for the deer, but they found no tracks. Mountain Lion said, "Where is Fox? Let him try to find the deer." Fox went to the south end of the world. Then he went around the world. He went to the place where the sun sets. Then he returned home. He told the people that he had seen no deer.

Then again Fox, together with Crow, journeyed through the hills in search of deer. Fox returned, but Crow did not. The people sent Eagle and some of the people with him to find Crow, but they returned without having found Crow or the tracks of the deer.

Next, Mountain Lion went, then the second Crow, then Mountain Quail, but they all saw nothing. Finally, the people sent the second Crow again with instructions to remain two days in the hills to see if he could find his brother. The second Crow climbed to the top of

117

"After Mountain Lion had everything ready, he sent his son inside the cave to kill the deer while he stayed outside." —Courtesy William Perry, istockphotos

a high mountain. The sun rose after he reached the summit. Then he looked down the mountain and saw a large cave. He returned home and told the people, "I think the deer are in that cave." He returned to the hill and he saw the deer entering the cave after sundown.

The chiefs assembled the people and they gave a dance. All of the people, all of the hunters assembled. Chief Mountain Lion put the people all around the cave in different places. He closed the exits of the cave. He placed the people all over the hills, so that they might kill the deer as they came forth from the cave.

After Mountain Lion had everything ready, he sent his son inside the cave to kill the deer. Young Mountain Lion went in to show his prowess. His father stayed outside. Then young Mountain Lion commenced to fight with the deer, but he fainted from the heat within the cave. His father entered and brought him out and laid him beside the stream. While he was rescuing his son, the deer escaped.

The chief said to his people, "Let us go home." Some of the people said to the chief, "We do not think that we shall reach home; we are starving." Then the chief went alone. While proceeding along the creek, the chief met Skunk. Skunk said to the chief, "Let me ride on your back. Give me a ride on your back and I will save some of your people."

The chief told Skunk to hang on tight. He said, "I am going to wade this river." Skunk said, "I do not care if all your people die, so long as I get this ride on your back across the river." The chief became angry when Skunk said that. When they reached the middle of the river, the chief pretended to stumble. He fell down and Skunk lost his hold. Skunk drowned. The chief went on across the river.

As soon as he had crossed the river, he looked up the hill. He saw the first Crow descending the hill with a load of deer. Crow told the chief, "I killed many deer on the creek."

The chief told Crow about all of the people who had died. "That is Skunk's fault," said the chief. "He told me he would save my people."

Crow said, "Your remaining people will be saved, for we have plenty of meat now."

—Adapted from Edward W. Gifford, *Miwok Myths.*[1]

THE GREATER MIWOK TERRITORY WAS LARGE; linguistically, it was the largest in California. It reached, in separated pockets, from the shores of Clear Lake to the Marin County coast; from the San Francisco Bay inland to portions of the Sacramento River delta; and along the Sierra's west side from the

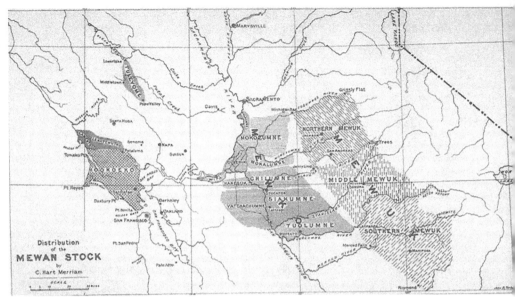

Map of Miwok groups —Adapted from "Myths Depicted by Demming and Hittel," C. Hart Merriam collection, University of California, Berkeley, and A. L. Kroeber, *Handbook of the Indians of California*

Mokelumne River to the Fresno River. Such a large and scattered people had few political or cultural ties with one another; there was no Miwok "nation" as such. As with the Monache, the main Miwok political unit was the village. Extended-family groupings and villages considered themselves autonomous, and many of their cultural customs reflected those of their closest non-Miwok neighbors. When Miwok bands visited each other, they might talk of common interests—of food gathering and preparation, hunts and games, children and friends, special ceremonies, and daily problems—but the cultural practices that guided their lives had different characteristics and meanings.

The Lake and Coastal Miwok were separated far from the Sierra foothill bands, though they were distant relatives with a common ancestral background. The Plains Miwok, a densely populated group of people with social patterns adapted to life in the central California valleys, resided to the west and north of the Sierra Miwok. The Yosemite people were an isolated Miwok subgroup whose beliefs and customs heavily intertwined with those of the Eastern Monache, who lived across the Sierra crest.

The highly political and socially organized Yokuts people lived to the south of the Sierra Miwok. To the northwest, the Wintun disseminated their ritualistic religious practices throughout central California. Directly north were the territorial Maidu, a smaller group of Penutians with a dialectically diverse language base and customs that often reflected the Hokan and Athabascan influence of cultures even farther north. The Hokan-derived Washoe lived to the northeast. To the south and east were the Eastern and Western Monache and the Owens Valley Paiute, all of whom had distinct Shoshonean languages and cultural ties.

The territory of the Sierra Miwok contained three principal groups with different Penutian-based dialects. The drainages of the Mokelumne and Calaveras rivers comprised what anthropologists classify as Northern Miwok. The Central Miwok lived south of them, in the Stanislaus and Tuolumne drainages, while the Southern Miwok settled along the Merced, Mariposa, and Chowchilla river drainages and the north side of the Fresno River drainage. Two families might be related, but if one lived on the Stanislaus River and the other lived on the Fresno, they would have a slightly different accent, pronounce words differently, and use their own slang expressions. Most foothill Miwok were multilingual.

Where a family lived defined who they were to all their neighbors. There was no designated name for each group, so people who lived north of a

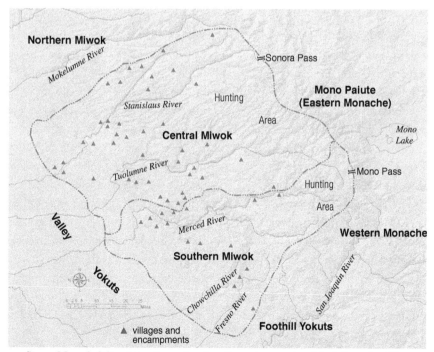

Sierra Nevada Miwok territory, showing the major groups with their main village sites —Adapted from A. L. Kroeber, *Handbook of the Indians of California*

given village were simply called northerners, and those who lived south were southerners, whether they were Miwok or not.

Of all the people of the southern High Sierra region, the Miwok were the most ritualistic. Influenced both by their historic Miwok culture and the ceremonies of their surrounding neighbors, they incorporated diverse customs and rites into their lives. Rituals varied from group to group, and even from village to village. The farther south a Miwok band lived, the greater was the influence of the Yokuts people, while farther north, the influence of the Maidu was greater.

EARLY MIGRATIONS OF THE MIWOK evidently progressed from north to south, with the central and southern dialects separating from the northern around 900 to 600 years ago. This was during the same moist, cool period in which the Western Monache moved from the eastern deserts into the Yokuts foothill areas. As the migrations continued, there is evidence the southern Miwok bands moved into Yokuts territory as recently as 750 to 450 years ago.

The life zone in which each Miwok group settled determined the form their daily existence would take. Each village adopted whatever subsistence pattern was most useful in its particular environment. Two villages could exist on the hillsides of the Stanislaus River drainage, yet if one family settled around today's Angel's Camp and another settled just 2,000 feet higher, above Murphy's Camp, their survival strategy and way of life would be different.

The family in the lower village would have access to all the resources of the foothills from the 1,000- to 3,000-foot elevation. This was the level where most Miwok villages existed, along streams that meandered through broad meadows and the gentle hills that blocked most of the dense Central Valley fogs in winter.

The lower hills were dotted with buckeyes, blue oaks, and live-oaks, which provided major food sources. Across the higher slopes, gray pines supplied timber and bark for the construction of homes. There were reeds and grasses to thatch roofs and weave baskets; clay to stabilize and weatherproof housing structures; river stones for ax heads and hammerheads; steatite to carve into dishes, pipes, arrow straighteners, and ornaments; granite for bedrock mortars and grinding implements; and an abundance of wildlife that provided not only meat but also bones for making needles, fish spears, awls, knife handles, and ornaments.

Food sources were abundant. Small game such as brush rabbits, jack-rabbits, raccoons, lampreys, and valley quail populated the foothills; whitefish and suckers filled the streams; and salmon could be procured in trade with the nearby Valley Miwok or Yokuts. Deer thrived on the chaparral-covered south-facing hillsides, while antelope roamed just a few miles downstream. Plant foods proliferated as well. Clover and bulbs were abundant, and tobacco plants were easy to propagate.

Winters in the lower elevations were green and mild, so it usually took only a rabbit-skin blanket or duck-feather or goose-feather bedding to ward off the chill. The summers were hot and dry, but if a village stood by a good spring or a perennial stream, life was relatively easy.

Families that settled just 2,000 feet higher, at 4,000- or 5,000-foot elevations, enjoyed cooler summers but also colder winters, often with snow. People in these villages used heavy fur blankets and wore deerskin skirts and trousers. Water was more plentiful here than at the lower elevations, but even smaller streams could be swift and difficult to reach. Travel was more difficult in the higher elevations, with steeper canyons, impenetrable chaparral, talus-covered slopes, and cliffs. It could take an hour to climb from the bottom of the Stanislaus River to a village high on the edge of the canyon.

Miwok occupation area in the foothill area of the Stanislaus River
—Photo by G. K. Gilbert (1905), courtesy USGS Photographic Library

Higher elevation occupation area along the Stanislaus River —Photo by G. K. Gilbert (1905), courtesy USC Photographic Library

Still, the resources were plentiful. Forests of yellow pines, incense cedars, and giant sequoias provided wood and bark for homes, as well as chrysalides to roast. There were acorns here, too, mostly from golden cup oaks, canyon live-oaks, and black oaks, and just a few miles up, sugar-pine nuts could be harvested. Mountain tubers, roots, greens, and berries were abundant; trout filled the streams, rivers, and lakes; and mule deer, gray squirrel, mountain quail, and pigeons inhabited the forests. Though it took more effort to live at the higher elevations, it was the favored home of several Miwok bands.

PEOPLE IN ALL SIERRA MIWOK COMMUNITIES had much in common. Conformance was the rule. The innovator and individualist had almost no place in Miwok society, and neither did the egotist, the boaster, or the aggressor. To be contemplative and reserved, to carefully follow custom and ritual was ideal.

Many customs were universal among all Sierra Miwok groups. Adults participated in their community's daily affairs without the management of a specific headman or chief. Everyone lived in settlements where all the men were related, family lines were patrilineal, and the belief system was a strict moiety in which everything came in twos and were opposites. All things belonged to one or the other of two halves of the world. There was sky and earth, land and water, a dry season and a wet one, heat and cold, light and dark, man and woman, young and old. The Miwok were descended from a mythical animal people who came from either the land or the water, so there were land people and there were water people, their personal line descended through the father.

To marry a person of the same moiety was strongly discouraged and subject to social criticism. There were restrictions on marrying relatives within your own lineage, but marriages between certain relatives of the opposite moiety could help foster family ties. In some villages, it was acceptable to marry one's first cousin, while in others it was frowned upon. A man who could afford it might have more than one wife, but this was rare, as it was difficult to gather enough wealth to support both.

Each moiety's members played important roles in the other moiety's functions. Counter moieties among the Central Miwok exchanged gifts at their *ahana* ceremony, and girls of opposite sides exchanged dresses at the time of their puberty ceremony. When someone died, women of the opposite moiety prepared the corpse and performed the ritual washing that concluded the annual mourning ceremony.

The steep terrain of the Tuolumne River flowing into a canyon —Photo by F. E. Matthes (c. 1914), courtesy USGS Photographic Library

All foothill and mountain groups—which included the Sierra Miwok, Maidu, and Western Mono—practiced both burial and cremation of the dead, depending on family and village customs and circumstances of locality. The Miwok believed, as did all peoples on the west side of the Sierra, that souls went to the western ocean.

The various Sierra Miwok groups performed many of the same ceremonies, though specific styles were adapted according to their area. All told the same tales generation after generation—moral tales involving animal characters and creation stories that never referred to ancient Miwok migrations, but rather honored the permanence of their winter home place.

VILLAGE LIFE WAS BUSY. There always was something to do. Men were occupied with hunting and fishing; making tools and weapons; building shelters with slab bark or grass thatch; and making routine repairs. Women and girls made and repaired baskets, pots, clothing and blankets, and had the daily subsistence chores of gathering and preparing food. Quamish (camas), soaproot, and swamp onion bulbs, harvested with three- or four-foot-long digging sticks of mountain mahogany or buckbrush, were an important part of meals.[2] The Sierra Miwok ate their first meal at sunrise, then the rest of the day each person ate whenever he or she was hungry. If there were guests, meals were served immediately upon their arrival, no matter what the hour.

Health issues took constant care. A hard physical existence created inevitable arthritis, tooth decay and periodontal diseases, tumors, broken bones, and assorted injuries. Illnesses and wounds were addressed with herbal remedies or a shaman's intervention, but these treatments could not always cure the problem. A Miwok could live to be forty or forty-five, but more than half of all babies died in infancy or childhood. Nevertheless, the Miwok were, according to early Yosemite resident Galen Clark, "strong, lean and agile, and the men are usually fine specimens of manhood." [3]

Beyond fulfilling basic daily needs, time was also set aside for art. The Miwok's preponderance of ceremonies and dances generated a high level of artistry. The intricate movements of the dances themselves were a form of artistic expression, as was the costuming for them. The men fashioned elaborate feathered regalia for each dance and ritual of their Bird and Kuksu cults. Both men and women created special bead and shell necklaces, belts, and ropes for other ceremonies and dances. The women also created art in their basketry. "While MiWok men found artistic expression in the intensity and transcendence of ceremonial dancing, MiWok women found their artistic expression in basket weaving," said Miwok tribal elder Ramona Dutschke in an interview. "To look closely at a Miwok basket in progress is hypnotic. Each small piece of the act is important in producing this effect."[4]

The body, too, was subject to artistic enhancement. Both men and women tattooed their bodies with straight lines that extended from chin to navel. This was accomplished by cutting the skin with a sharp piece of obsidian or flint and rubbing the cut with ashes. They also applied body paints for special ceremonies and dances in which both men and women participated. Galen Clark observed that Miwok men were "rather light in color, but frequently rub their bodies with some kind of oil, which gives the flesh a much redder and more glossy appearance. The hair is black and straight, and the eyes are black and deep set. The beard is sparse, and in former times was not allowed to grow at all, each hair being pulled out with a rude kind of tweezers."[5]

A flat skull, forehead, and nose were signs of beauty in the Sierra Miwok culture. What nature did not provide for a child, Miwok women attempted to create. An infant was assured a flat head in the back by being wrapped in its cradleboard for hours each day. Mothers molded a short, flat forehead by massaging the infant's head from center to sides, and the nose was shaped by pressing it in and rubbing the eyebrows apart.

Young people between twelve and fifteen years of age had their ears and nasal septum pierced; the openings were made progressively larger by inserting increasingly thicker grass stems. The women favored earrings of beads and shells, while the men wore large earplugs of bird bone with white feathers protruding from the ends, and nose sticks made of polished bone or shell. The most popular ear ornaments for young girls and boys were flowers inserted into their pierced ears. Flowers were a favorite accessory

Body cleanliness and decoration were important to the Miwok. The soaproot plant was used as a cleaning agent, and its roots were made into brushes.
—Courtesy Tulare County Museum

for everyone, especially showy blooms placed in their hair. The hair was kept shiny, washed every few days with the lather of soaproot plant and groomed with a soaproot-fiber brush.

WHILE THE VARIOUS MIWOK GROUPS had much in common, there were also many cultural differences between the Central and Southern Sierra Miwok. A Central Miwok family on the Stanislaus River and a Southern Miwok family on the Fresno could be of the same moiety, and each member would be called by his or her representative animal name, but that name could be different in each village. On the Stanislaus, a land person could be called frog and a water person jay, while on the Fresno, they might be called coyote and grizzly.

Rituals and ceremonies could also vary significantly between the two divisions. With the Central Miwok, most ceremonies reflected the influence of their northern Patwin, Nisinan, and Maidu neighbors and revolved around the Kuksu cult, with its impersonations of various gods, spirits, and ghosts. Their observances were filled with dance and ritual, especially when cremating bodies and before war. Central Miwok often made special food offerings and observed food taboos connected with the ceremonies.

Important ceremonies were called by a village chief, often to prevent an impending disaster heralded by a dream. Set protocols were followed carefully, especially in the dances, for harm could befall both the dancers and the audience if they were not. This was not because a special spirit or god might be offended, but rather because an impersonal supernatural power would automatically create a problem if the required movements were not made. In keeping with the northern traditions, the Central Miwok held their major gatherings indoors, in large, semisubterranean roundhouses that reverberated with the beat of northwest-style wooden foot drums.

In contrast, Southern Miwok ceremonies centered around the bird cult, adopted from the Yokuts, with its outdoor pota ceremony that featured bird costumes and live avian guardians. Raptors had high spiritual status among the Southern Miwok, Yokuts, and Western Mono. The eagle, condor, and prairie falcon were regarded as sacred chiefs. The birds were captured and put in the custody of human chiefs of the appropriate totemic lineage, who directed their care, sacrifice, and burial.

Adult condors were killed for use in dance ceremonies. In at least one spirit-impersonating dance, the entire skin of the condor was worn. The birds' bodies were cremated in a ritualistic ceremony that included dances, singing, and throwing offerings of seeds on the pyre. Eagles and falcons enjoyed a more fortunate fate. In the case of eagles, only certain feathers were plucked for decorating dance aprons, capes, and other ceremonial regalia. Prairie falcons were neither killed nor plucked. Only molted feathers could be collected at roosting places, for it was forbidden to molest these birds. Live falcons were captured and held as an important part of the pota ceremony. After the ceremony, they were released or passed on to another village for use in its own pota.

Ritual was an important part of bird capture and care. Young eagles were taken from the nest when they were about ready to fly. A feast preceded their capture, staged by a number of men and women beneath the tree or cliffs where the nest was located. Participants scattered seeds and beads as offerings, for the eagle was believed to be endowed with supernatural powers, and if the proper offerings were not made, the eagle catcher might meet with misfortune.

Whenever the young eagles needed to be moved, they were carried like human infants in cradleboards on the caretaker's back. "Each eagle was believed to be like a man and to have likes and dislikes," ethnologist Edward F. Gifford wrote. "From certain men he would not take food, but if he liked the man who was offering him food he would shake his wings and take the food. Such a man was then delegated by the chief to feed the eagles."[6]

The golden eagle played an important role in the Southern Miwok bird cult. —Courtesy Yykkaa, Dreamstime

The Central Sierra Miwok eventually adapted bird cult traditions into their culture, too. The pota ceremony, probably the Miwok's most important ritual, was practiced by both the Southern and Central groups. Southern Miwok potas pit opposing moieties against each other in mock battles intended to settle grievances. Disputes settled in a pota were usually serious ones, such as the murder of a kinsman, a leader's unkind words about a person's abilities, or a shaman causing illness or death through magic.

The ceremony was held outdoors in a large clearing, where two or three long poles were erected. One pole always held a bearskin, while the other one or two bore rude tule effigies of dead individuals of one lineage. The participants were divided into two groups according to moiety. The group that represented the moiety of the effigies gathered to defend them, while the opposing moiety sang malevolent songs, shot arrows at the effigies, and tried to pull them down and destroy them. Any dogs that ventured into the clearing were shot with arrows, too. Presiding over all sat captured prairie falcons. The ceremony could not be held without them, and once they were captured, the pota had to take place or sickness would engulf the lineage that held the birds.

In the Central Sierra, some potas did not include effigies and did not define which moiety was being attacked, so all the participants sang the malevolent songs and learned only after the ceremony which lineage was being reviled. When the Central Miwok adopted bird cult ceremonies, they put more emphasis on ritual, observing food taboos, instilling ceremonial dress with deeper importance, and placing an emphasis on feathers, a symbol evidently carried over from the ancient bird cults of southern California. Elaborate feather robes and headdresses were endowed with supernatural powers; mishandling them could cause sickness in either the performers or the audience, so they were kept in the custody of a special shaman. For the less ritualistic Southern Miwok, the feather regalia held no sanctity, so each dancer kept his or her own costume.

Both the central and southern Sierra groups held two types of gatherings—the sacred, or spiritual, and the "profane." The sacred ceremonies were those connected with the Kuksu and bird cults, mourning rites, and rituals to prevent an impending disaster—all of which required elaborate paraphernalia. Such events were held in the larger villages of important ceremonial chiefs, with people from smaller villages attending.

Contrasting the spiritual ceremonies were profane dances, held purely for celebration. These were held on many occasions, often within the smaller communities. They could be held in conjunction with the more serious ceremonies held at the start of hunting and fishing seasons and at the acorn harvest, but a gathering could also be organized on other occasions deemed worthy of a celebration, such as puberty observances or the conclusion of a successful hunt.

Although the particulars of these events were slightly different among the Miwok groups, in general they were communal parties devoted to all-night dancing, sports contests, gambling, and feasting, with singers, dancers, and ribald clowns. The dances consisted of a prescribed foot shuffling and stomping by the men, and a sideways swaying motion of the women, circling a central fire. The beat of a foot drum or clapstick rattle and the rising and falling chants of women filled the air. The Southern Miwok usually held the festivities in an outdoor clearing. In the central Sierra, women and children were allowed into the ceremonial roundhouses, which were otherwise taboo for them.

In addition to the variations in ceremonies were other differences between the southern and central groups. Some of the Central Miwok learned to make the crude pottery vessels of the Western Monache, who learned the technique from the Owens Valley Paiute. Many of the Southern Miwok crafted the utilitarian oaken bowls of their Yokuts neighbors, and like the Yokuts cooked in steatite vessels over fires or boiled soups and mushes with heated chunks of steatite dropped into tightly woven baskets.

The Central Miwok practiced annual fall burning of both foothill and mountain chaparral to destroy less productive older growth and encourage the growth of new plants and grasses, as did their Maidu neighbors and most native groups who lived in forested areas. They seeded tobacco, as the Eastern Mono and Paiute people did, but they did not cultivate it as some other groups did. They also logged timber for building homes and lodges, their lumbering methods having been handed down from the forest-dwelling people of the north. In contrast, the Southern Miwok lived mostly in woven grass huts or oak-framed structures covered with shrub branches, as the foothill Yokuts did.

Miwok wood and bark houses. Depending on elevation, buildings were made of woven grasses, shrub-covered wood frames, or timbers covered with bark.
—Illustration by Jana Botkin, Cabin Arts

THE MIWOK TRADED EXTENSIVELY with their neighbors in all directions. Even the desert Paiute, who were distrusted by most western Sierra people, were closely involved in trade with the Central Miwok, and some intermarriage took place. Coastal trade was also important. Both the Central and Southern Sierra Miwok traveled annually to the ocean to gather shells and feast on seafood.

The Sierra Miwok had elaborate social and cultural structures to maintain peace within their own groups and among trading partners, but territorial claims, prejudices against foreigners, and fear of other peoples' motivations created quarrels, enemies, and sometimes battles. There was even alienation between the Central and Southern Sierra Miwok due to the Central Miwok belief that southern people had supernatural poisoning abilities. The pota ceremony, with its battles over raised effigies that represented foes, released some of this constant fear, but it did not extinguish it. Vague fears and hostility were ever-present, as described by ethnologist A. L. Kroeber:

> By impulse, the native is thoroughly peaceable. A plan of spoliation or oppression rarely enters his mind. But suspicion is ever gnawing within him. Punctilious as he is not to commit a deliberate offense, he constantly conceives that others have wished him ill and worked the contemplated injury. And so he spends his life in half-concealed bad will, in non-intercourse, in plotting with more or less open magic, or occasionally in an open feud. He has always been wronged by some one, and is always planning a merited but dark punishment.[7]

Such dark imaginings, fears, and actual trespasses evidently resulted in some major conflicts. During archaeological excavations conducted between 1967 and 1972 in the Chowchilla River basin, several Southern Miwok cemetery excavations revealed that nearly half of the adult men buried there had met violent deaths. "The numerous arrow and spear points found deeply imbedded in skulls and other bones clearly indicate that warfare (or perhaps intra-village feuding) was commonplace in prehistoric times."[8]

In spite of such evidence, the Sierra Miwok were not considered a warring group by other Sierra tribes. They were an adaptive people, assimilating many rituals and traditions from cultures north and south of them. They traded often with the Monache and Yokuts, shared some hunting grounds, and lived in general harmony with their related neighbors in Yosemite Valley.

10. The Yosemite

THE LEGEND OF TO-TAU-KON-NU'-LA and TIS-SA'-AK
A Yosemite Tale

Innumerable moons and snows have passed since the Great Spirit guided a little band of his favorite children into the beautiful vale of Ah-wah'-ne. They prospered and built other towns outside of Ah-wah'-ne, and became a great nation. They learned wisdom by experience and by observing how the Great Spirit taught the animals and insects to live, and they believed that their children could absorb the cunning of the wild creatures.

And so the young son of their chieftain was made to sleep in the skins of the beaver and coyote, that he might grow wise in building and keen of scent in following game. On some days he was fed fish that he might become a good swimmer, and on other days the eggs of the great crane that he might grow tall and keen of sight and have a clear ringing voice. He was also fed on the flesh of the deer that he might be fleet of foot, and on that of the great grizzly bear, Yo-sem'-i-te, to make him powerful in combat.

The little boy grew up and became a great and wise chieftain. As was the custom, his name was changed from time to time as his

"After a time, Choo'-too-se-ka' built himself a great house on the summit of the rock and had a chair where on all festival occasions he could overlook and talk to the great multitude below."
—Photo of El Capitan by C. E. Carleton (ca. 1880–85), courtesy Bancroft Library, University of California, Berkeley

character developed, until he was called Choo'-too-se-ka', the Supreme Good. His grand house was built at the base of the great rock called To-tau-kon-nu'-la [now called El Capitan] because the great cranes made their nests and raised their young in a meadow at its summit.

As the moons and snows passed, this great rock and all the great rocky walls around the valley grew in height, and the hills became high mountains. After a time, Choo'-too-se-ka' built himself a great house on the summit of the rock and had a chair where on all festival occasions he could overlook and talk to the great multitude below. The remains of his chair are still to be seen.

Choo'-too-se-ka' was then named To-tau-kon-nu'-la because he had built his house on the summit of the great rock. He had no wife, but all the women served him in his domestic needs. The donations which he received from his people at the great annual festivals made him wealthy and he gave freely to the needy.

One day, while standing on the top of the great dome above the south wall of the valley [Sentinel Dome], he saw some strange people approaching, bearing heavy burdens. They were fairer of skin and their clothing was different, and when they drew near, he asked them who they were.

A woman replied, "I am Tis-sa'-ak, and these are some of my people. We come from far south. I have heard of your great wisdom and goodness, and have come to see you and your people. We bring you presents of many fine baskets and beads of many colors as tokens of our friendship. When we have rested and seen your people and beautiful valley we will return to our home."

To-tau-kon-nu'-la was much pleased with his fair visitor and built a large house for her and her companions on the summit of the great dome at the east end of the valley [Half Dome]. She tarried there and taught the women of Ah-wah'-ne how to make beautiful baskets. To-tau-kon-nu'-la visited her daily and wanted her to remain and be his wife, but she denied him, saying, "I must return to my people." When he still persisted, she left in the night and was never seen again.

The love-stricken chieftain forgot his people and went in search of her, but they never saw him again. Many moons afterward, there appeared on the face of the great rock To-tau-kon-nu'-la the figure of a man in a flowing robe, with one hand extended toward the west. At about the same time, the face of the beautiful Tis-sa'-ak, with her dark hair cut straight across her forehead and falling down at the sides, appeared on the great flat side of the dome where she had resided.

—Adapted from Galen Clark,
Indians of the Yosemite and Vicinity.[1]

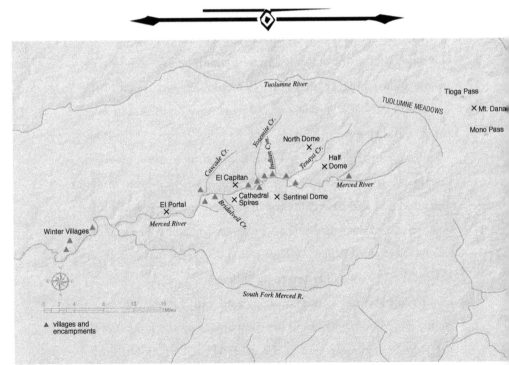

Yosemite territory, showing major villages and campsites. Yosemite territory had no strict boundarie or designated hunting grounds.

EXACTLY WHO FIRST SETTLED IN THE YOSEMITE AREA IS UNKNOWN. While there is some evidence that people visited the Yosemite region as early as 5,000 to 7,500 years ago, it was not until around 4,000 to 4,500 years ago that trans-Sierra trade appeared in the area. Some of the people who lived in the Mono Lake area resettled in the Tuolumne and Merced river drainages, and they may have ventured into the valley. The Yosemite area appears to have originally been a summer hunting and trading ground with only seasonal encampments, but sometime around 1500 to 1000 BC, permanent settlements were occupied for the majority of the year.

After the arrival of the first prehistoric settlers, several groups of Miwok people migrated from the west into the Yosemite region around AD 500, bringing distinct changes in tools with them. Obsidian points became smaller, indicating the introduction of the bow and arrow, and stone mortars replaced milling stones. Five or six hundred years later, around AD 1000 to 1200, other cultural changes took place: projectile points became even smaller; local soapstone bowls and beads were manufactured; and clamshell disc beads and abalone shell ornaments appeared from trade with coastal people. It was during this time that the Central and Southern Miwok dialects began to evolve from the northern dialects.

The Miwok evidently remained in Yosemite Valley during the Little Ice Age, which lasted for over two hundred years. Even in a colder climate, the advantages of living in the valley were many. The valley's relative isolation protected residents from incursions from outsiders, and wildlife was able to survive year-round at the 4,000-foot elevation. In most years, winter snowfall was light on the valley floor, so only the coldest months were spent in the foothills downstream. Large winter villages were established along the Merced River at El Portal, on a ridge near Bull Creek, at Hite's Cove, and at several lower sites along the Tuolumne River, but some villages in Yosemite Valley remained occupied year-round. The permanent Miwok settlers of the valley eventually developed a distinct culture of their own, and they came to be known as the Ahwahnechee.

ALL EVIDENCE INDICATES that from AD 1200 to 1800, life for the Ahwahnechee changed very little. Living in the Sierra rain zone under dense forests and along damp meadows, the Yosemite people constructed homes with good insulation. Most were conical structures made of pine poles covered with two to four overlapping layers of wind-resistant and rain-resistant incense-cedar bark, with willow or bay leaves often woven in as insect repellants. At night or in inclement weather, the inhabitants placed a large bark slab over the entry opening.

For greater warmth, the occupants sometimes heaped a layer of pine needles on the inside and a layer of earth on the outside of the shelter's lower portions. They often used a vented fire pit in the center of the structure. For seats and beds they piled leaves, pine needles, or sedges, covered with skins or fur blankets, with pine needles or rolled-up coyote skins for pillows. Baskets filled with food, implements, and materials were suspended from the interior walls. However, as with all people of the Sierra, the Yosemite Ahwahnechee used the houses only when necessary. In summer, bark and brush lean-tos provided open-air shelter from wind and sun. Usually one family occupied a house, which could accommodate up to six people as well as their dogs.

Several small encampments were settled along the Merced River in Yosemite Valley. The dwellings were made of cedar bark to repel wind and rain. —Courtesy Yosemite National Park archives

Dogs were an integral part of Miwok life. Of ancient breeding, they were usually medium-sized, brindled, prick-eared, and shorthaired, with a curled tail and a muzzle like a coyote. Dogs were a prized trade commodity, for they protected dwellings and food caches from wild cats and ground squirrels, ate refuse, helped in hunting forays, and, if winter rations ran short, they could be eaten.

Trade with other Indians made survival easier for all parties. The Yosemite Miwok offered sugar-pine nuts, meadow seeds, and salt in trade for gray-pine nuts, dried fish, and dried tobacco from lower foothill Miwok. With the Eastern Monache and Paiutes they traded

The procurement of nuts for trade and winter use required safe means of storage to protect against mold and animals. Elevated acorn caches dotted the valley floor. —Photo by C. Hart Merriam (n.d.), courtesy Bancroft Library, University of California, Berkeley

their acorns, manzanita berries, abalone shell ornaments, steatite, arrows, and basket materials in return for pine nuts, pandora moth larvae, Mono Lake brine-fly pupae, baskets, animal skins, salt, and obsidian. Not all trade items were strict necessities. Ceremonial objects such as shell ornaments, feathers, red and white earth for paint, and special animal skins were prized. Eastern Mono Paiute and Miwok women also traded baskets and basket materials, sharing and incorporating each other's designs and techniques.

Each trading session had certain protocols that were followed. At the beginning of each meeting, the Eastern Paiutes would present a "loaf" of salt to a Miwok chief to begin the exchange. As Yosemite historian Elizabeth O'Neill described it:

> Trading was a solemn ceremony of gift-giving. Each side knew what the other wanted, and the only problem was paying and receiving a just price. For instance, a Paiute Chief would present a Miwok

Chief with a large lump of salt. The Miwok would reciprocate with a basket of acorns, and the Paiute would then display some choice obsidian flakes for making arrowheads. Each "gift" was carefully gauged to evoke the return of an equivalent "gift" according to understood values. At the end of the series of elaborate transactions both parties returned home having completed that season's commerce.[2]

The Yosemite Miwok appear to have had more contact and trade with the Mono Lake people than with other neighboring groups. Tuolumne Meadows, which lay on the trans-Sierra Mono Trail, was one site where the Yosemite and Mono traders met in late summer. Entire families set up large campsites on rocky moraines, where they shared feasts, stories, and friendships. Sometimes a young Mono woman, or even a whole family, would extend a trading visit to spend a winter and occasionally several years in Yosemite Valley, and inevitably, intermarriages took place. Ahwahnechee trade and marriage ties with the Eastern Mono continued for generations.

A MONO BRIDE who came to live with the Yosemite people would be living in a far more populated place than her own homeland. The widespread Owens Valley and Mono Lake area supported only around thirty villages, about two thousand persons total, while the narrow Yosemite Valley is estimated to have had thirty-six to forty villages at one time, some with as many as one hundred people. Coming from desert lands, she would also have to adjust to the Sierra's rain belt. The air was damp in the Yosemite meadows most of the year, and

Tuolumne Meadows above Yosemite Valley was a major trading site with the Mono Paiute. Friendly intertribal relationships brought many Paiute to the valley; they often became permanent residents
—Photo by F. C. Calkins (1913), courtesy USGS Photographic Library

The largest Yosemite Valley village was Koom-i-ne, settled in the forest at the base of Yosemite Falls. —Photo by F. E. Matthes (1913), courtesy USGS Photographic Library

the small cedar-bark houses were not as airy or as fresh-smelling as the willow and grass structures of the eastern Sierra.

In some ways, life would be easier, for resources were far more plentiful on the west side of the Sierra crest than on the east. While most daily chores were universal throughout the Sierra, several Ahwahnechee customs were decidedly different. The Mono bride would have to learn to be more self-reliant, depending more on her husband's family than on the close-knit communities in which she was raised. The daybreak meal would be the only one she would serve and eat with the family, generally over a communal basket of acorn mush, each member dipping into the gruel with their first two fingers. For the rest of the day and evening, except on special occasions, everyone cooked and ate whenever they were hungry, snacking on greens, bulbs, and berries when they were in season, as well as various biscuits, soups, fish, and meats.

The young woman would also have to learn how to communicate with her new family, for the Eastern Mono language was almost totally unrelated to that of the Ahwahnechee. Coming from a loosely organized and mobile community, she would need to learn all the practices of a society based on totemic moieties, including who lived in which village and the animal designations that belonged to each one, with those on the north side, or "inside," of the Merced River having land moiety names, and those on the south, or "outside," having water names.

A wife often accompanied her husband and his family on trading excursions. Sometimes she would visit small outlying settlements, perhaps traveling as far as Little Yosemite Valley, above Nevada Falls. More often, especially on important occasions, she would visit the major villages, on the main valley floor. The largest was Koom-i-ne, three-quarters of a mile long, just below Yosemite Falls; east of it was Ah-wah'-ne, which claimed the largest tract of open, level land in the valley.[3] These two villages had large assembly and ceremonial houses where the Kuksu and bird dances were held. Inside each forty-foot-diameter semisubterranean structure was a five- to ten-foot-long foot drum that had been cut from the hollowed trunk of a white oak. When stamped upon, its vibrations in the resonant chamber of the large assembly house could be alarming to a newcomer.

The beauty and relative isolation of the Yosemite Valley promoted population growth.
—Photo by J. K. Hillers (1892), courtesy USGS Photographic Library

She would discover the power of rock in a valley filled with its presence, learning the names of the granite outcroppings that had been laid bare by glaciers and erosion. She would memorize the legends of Pu-si-na Chuk-ka, the rock that once had been a squirrel at its acorn cache; Tu-tok-a-nu-la, the measuring worm, which scaled the towering granite wall now known as El Capitan to rescue two bear cubs; Hum-mo, the Lost Arrow spire, where a betrothed man fell to his death after shooting the arrow as a message to his bride.[4]

WHILE THE NATURAL WORLD WAS AN ESSENTIAL PART OF LIFE, the supernatural world also played a major role. The Yosemite had an intricate belief system composed of spirits and supernatural powers that resided not only in the rocks, but in every material thing. "These Indians believe that everything on earth, both natural and artificial, is endowed with an immortal spirit, which is indestructible," Galen Clark wrote.[5] Even the portable mortar was accorded a supernatural origin, its invention attributed to Coyote at the beginning of time.

These spirits often acted as avengers. If a person committed a crime, did not follow a certain protocol, or harmed someone or something, supernatural

From the Yosemite highlands down to the valley floor, rock dominated the landscape, shaping prehistoric culture. —Photo by F. E. Matthes (1913), courtesy USGS Photographic Library

forces might instill poison in the culprit, causing illness. Others avoided him until they were persuaded that he had appeased the spirits with good acts. Even then, the offender worried on the monthly anniversary of his crime, fearful that the spirits might punish him by depriving him of health, food, or sleep.

Even if no was crime committed, an ailment could be inflicted by a jealous or angry relative or neighbor, an enemy, or a hostile shaman. Whatever their causes, almost all illnesses could be cured only with the aid of supernatural forces. Only the powers of a shaman, a spiritual healer who had derived his or her powers from spirits, could cure disease. The shaman accomplished the healing through dancing, singing, manipulation of the patient's body, meditation, dreams, herbal remedies, or sucking out the poison that inhabited the patient.

The shaman's power was usually inherited patrilineally. The dream, or calling, came through a young man or woman's dream or through a conscious vision quest, with the dream or vision determining what kind of shaman he or she would be. It could be bear, coyote, rattlesnake, weather, or a host of other forms derived from the powers of the natural world. The novice shaman learned the skills and secrets of his position from an experienced shaman of the same calling, most often a relative. According to ethnologist Eugene L. Conrotto, even the "poison shaman" had to be taught his trade:

> A man's father, when he begins to make him a poison shaman, places a crystal in the left hand of his son. After placing it there, he makes him eat the root of a plant with poisonous properties. The father takes his son into the brush. He does not eat anything for a day. He gives him porcupine quills, and he sticks a feather into the ground at a distance.
>
> "Hit that!" he says, "Hit that!" giving him the porcupine quills. He shoots the feather with the porcupine quills. Then he scatters earth upon it, and he calls the feather by name, as he scatters earth upon it.

Such a shaman's life was not an easy one, as Conrotto points out:

> A man who is a poisoner must live far away from everyone. He must go out there near the place where he is living, and when he gets there he rolls a log about. He shouts, he hates to let his poison go. The poison is like fire. He calls the name of the one he is poisoning. He commands the poison. "Go to his head!" he says. Sometimes he

says, "Go to his breast!" To whatever place is mentioned, there goes the poison.

After poisoning and killing someone, he cries for the man more than anyone. He grieves for the one he kills.[6]

As a medium for the earth's spirits, the shaman's struggle between destructive and healing forces in the isolated Yosemite Valley was intense. Floods, avalanches, severe cold spells, meadow-searing droughts—all required interventions and appeasement of the spirits. Those same spirits also guided the Ahwahnechee's relationships with their neighbors—including the Paiute, who lived beyond the High Sierra summit.

11. The Paiute

HY-NAN-NU
An Owens Valley Paiute Tale

Once there lived two orphan boys. The younger, Hy-nan-nu, was so small that he was yet in his basket cradle. The older brother carried him when he went hunting for deer and quail. The infant grew fast and the older boy built a tight wigwam in which to keep him. One day Hy-nan-nu got out and went to the end of the world, where he found many smooth rocks. He returned and the brother bade him go and bring some of the rocks back.

The brother made a bow of wood and arrows from the rocks, and Hy-nan-nu used them to kill a bear. The next day he saw his grandmothers and tried to shoot them. When they fled into their tonis [dwellings], he smashed their baskets. Seeing his mischief, they pursued and killed him. The brother knew what had happened, and on coming to where the boy's body was, he struck it with a stick. Hy-nan-nu jumped up good as new and with his bow and arrows killed his grandmothers, then they came to life again.[1] Hy-nan-nu broke their baskets again, and when they pursued him, he jumped into a cave, twisted up in the air, and killed them again.

Then the brother took him to see his grandfathers, the bears. The bears were pulling down the tops of pine trees, and then by holding on as the tops sprang back, they were thrown high into the air. Hy-nan-nu wanted such a ride, but he could not sing so as to protect himself, and when he came down he changed into a rock. When the brother made him alive again, Hy-nan-nu induced the bears to be shot into the air from the tree, and they became rocks as they fell. Soon the rocks again changed to bears, who chased Hy-nan-nu and

"The bears were pulling down the tops of pine trees, and then by holding on as the tops sprang back, they were thrown high into the air." —Courtesy Randy Hjelsand, Dreamstime

caught him and killed him, leaving only a small drop of blood under the leaves.

When his brother again restored him, he asked him to go see his grandmothers, who were now tiny creatures in the water. The lake began to rise up to the tops of the trees, and Hy-nan-nu ran up the mountain, but the water followed him. His brother told him to throw a rock into a hole in the air. As Hy-nan-nu threw the rock he caught hold of it and was drawn upward. The water continued to rise and fell on him through the hole in the air, but, finally beaten, it went down.

When night came the brother built a fire on which he put a deer. When they looked again the deer was gone. One after another they killed all the deer and put them on the fire, and one after another the deer went under the fire and disappeared. They took a great stick and moved all the deer from under the fire. Out came a great man who chased them all over the world until they fell down dead and could not come to life again.

—Adapted from W. A. Chalfant, *The Story of Inyo*, from a narration written by an Eastern Mono Indian.[2]

THE PAIUTE PEOPLE OF THE EASTERN SIERRA were transplants from ancient cultures. Descended from early migrating populations who moved from midcontinent into the unglaciated Great Basin ranges as early as 25,000 years ago, they followed a nomadic way of life that depended on big-game hunting. By 15,000 to 10,000 years ago, the Great Basin was a prime location for habitation. Archaeologist Charles W. Campbell described it as lush: "During the Ice Age, the weather of the Great Basin was very moist due to its close proximity to the glacial ice sheets. There were verdant grasslands where dusty sage flats now exist, and many vast lakes and lake chains filled by the bountiful rains of the period."[3]

As the climate warmed 9,000 to 7,000 years ago, the herds of large ice-age animals began to disappear, and the nomadic Great Basin people gradually learned to depend more on smaller animals and plant foods. They settled in small familial groupings scattered throughout widely separated water basins and meadowlands surrounded by vast deserts. Although separated from each other geographically, these early Paiute groups were considered one people by later ethnologists and archaeologists, as their languages were based on the same Numic foundations and were mutually intelligible. At one time, they occupied West Coast lands all the way from the Cascade Mountains south to Mexico.

With a mild climate, plentiful water, and varied food resources, the valleys along the east side of the southern Sierra Nevada became favored settlement areas. Artifacts of basalt spear points provide evidence that people hunted in the Great Basin around 10,000 years ago. By 9,500 years ago, they were crossing the Sierra Nevada to hunt on the western slopes, creating trails that later became important trade routes.

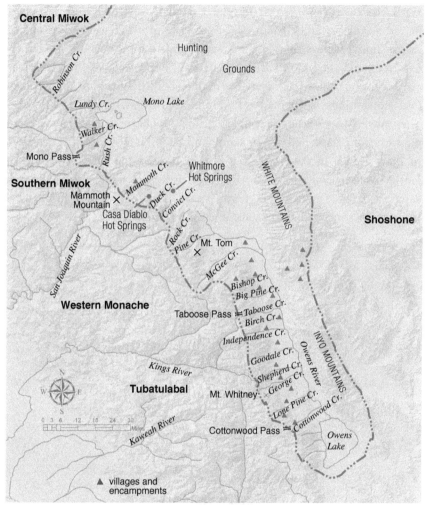

Eastern Sierra Paiute territory, with major features and boundaries

The Paiute who moved west from the Great Basin to the lowland valley below the High Sierra's eastern escarpment have been classified as Owens Valley Paiute. Those who migrated from the north along the east side of the Sierra Nevada became known as the Paviotso, or Northern Paiute. The Northern Paiute who settled along the high desert valleys and plateaus north of Owens Valley are now known as Eastern Monache, Eastern Mono, or Mono Paiute. The Eastern Monache who lived in the Mono Lake region were called the Kuzedika, later classified as the Mono Lake Paiute.

WINTERS COULD BE HARD for the Eastern Monache Paiute who lived in the 5,000- to 10,000-foot elevations. The growing season was shorter in the higher valleys than in the lowlands, with fewer deer and productive oak trees, and the piñon harvest was always unpredictable. Still, the Eastern Monache utilized the available resources fully. They built their villages near hot springs in the hills of Mammoth Mountain, and Long Valley. They moved often throughout their territory and beyond, crossing the Sierra crest to camp, hunt, and gather acorns in Hetch Hetchy Valley. If deer were in short supply in the Mono Basin, they crossed the summit to hunt in Little Yosemite Valley. Within their local area, they augmented their meat supply with gray squirrels, sage grouse, small birds, marmots, black-tailed jackrabbits, cottontail rabbits, and snowshoe hares.

Rabbit-skin robes were essential Paiute garments from November through April, when bitter winds swept down from the Sierra Nevada crest. —Courtesy Special Collections, University of Nevada, Reno, Library

The Mono Lake Paiute held frequent jackrabbit drives on the lake's north shore, utilizing them for food and blankets. Their most important resources were large quantities of obsidian, brine shrimp, brine flies, and edible moths that bred in an immense Jeffrey pine forest south of the lake. The obsidian, a

Obsidian from Glass Mountain in the Mono Paiute territory had high trade value as blanks for making arrowheads and spear points.
—Courtesy Inyo National Forest archives

natural volcanic glass found at Glass Mountain and surrounding volcanic domes, was formed from rhyolite flows that rose from the Long Valley Caldera 680,000 to 630,000 years ago. Composed of 75 to 77 percent silica, it was some of the finest obsidian in the world. Used for arrowheads and tools, it was a prized trade item throughout central California.

While Owens Lake had its share of brine shrimp and brine flies, it was Mono Lake that supplied these food resources not only to Mono Basin residents, but also to visitors from surrounding areas. Late summer found groups of Owens Valley, eastern Shoshone, northern Washoe, Western Monache, Miwok, and even Yokuts groups camping on the lake's shores to harvest kutsavi, the pupae of the brine fly, *Ephydra hians*.[4] At times, the flies bred in such great numbers in Mono Lake that the pupae rose to the surface in clusters that resembled islands of worms.

As the pupae washed ashore and collected in natural windrows, women waded into the water and scooped up hundreds of bushels of them onto flat

A gull feeds on white clusters of Mono Lake brine fly pupae, which the Eastern Monache also enjoyed eating. —Courttesy Jay 0110, Flickr Creative Commons

baskets. Some of the harvested larvae were cooked fresh in boiling water and eaten with acorn or pine-nut mush, but most of them were laid out to dry in the sun. The women rubbed the dried larvae between their palms to loosen the thin outer membrane and tossed them in a winnowing basket to separate the meat from the chaff. The dried kutsavi was an important winter protein source for the Eastern Monache, supplementing their caches of nuts and dried seeds. According to some historians, kutsavi was so valuable to the Kuzedika that warfare could ensue if one group infringed upon the worm claim of another.[5] Long after Euro-American foods were introduced to the local Paiute, the greasy, somewhat bitter kutsavi maintained its importance as a delicacy.

The other resource regarded as a delicacy was *pe'-ag'gie*, the larvae of the pandora moth.[6] While most Sierra people gathered pupae of various moths, the immature pandora moth was considered a specialty. The Western Monache ate the parched chrysalides, while the Eastern Monache relished them in their caterpillar stage. When word was received that the caterpillars had hatched, whole villages dropped their work and went to the pe'-ag'gie grounds. For weeks, families camped in the Jeffrey pine forests that grew profusely in the

Pe'-ag'gie trees in the Jeffrey pine forests of Mono Paiute territory. Note the remnants of trench around the trees to capture pandora moth caterpillars, which the Paiutes considered a delicac
—Courtesy Bureau of Land Management, Inyo

loose pumice soil between Mono and Mammoth Lakes. It was an important event, for the caterpillars emerge only once every two years.

In late June of their hatching years, hordes of the beautiful pandora moths deposit eggs in the bark of Jeffrey pines. When the tiny larvae hatch, they bunch together on the pine needles and feed on them. There they stay until the next summer, hibernating through the winter and then gorging on the needles in the spring and summer. By August, they are fat, furry, full-grown caterpillars, prime as a tasty treat. They start their journey down the trunk of the tree to bury themselves in the loose volcanic soil, where they will form a hard-cased cocoon that must last until they emerge as a new batch of moths the following June or July. It is during their movement down the trunk that they meet their fate as a delicacy.

To get ready for the harvest, the Eastern Monache made communal trips to the Jeffrey pine forests in July. Each family was assigned a specific area of trees. Around each tree they dug trenches with nearly vertical outer walls, two feet wide and ten to sixteen inches deep, completely encircling the base. As the caterpillars crawled down to the ground to pupate, they were trapped in the trenches, gathered by the people, and immediately baked alive in large mounds of dirt covered with burning wood. When the larvae had lost their hair and turned to a yellowish brown color, the fire was pushed aside. After the dirt had cooled, it was sieved through special baskets, and the morsels were laid out to air dry for several days. A small portion of the harvest was used in stews; the remainder was stored for the winter months. One American taster found the larvae tough and the stew "insipid from lack of salt, the flavor resembling to my palate the taste of linseed oil."[7]

THE OWENS VALLEY PAIUTE lived in a different environment from their Eastern Monache neighbors; theirs was essentially low foothills and desert wetlands. Although the two groups had the same language and basic culture, shared some hunting grounds, visited each other often, and intermarried frequently, the Owens Valley people's way of life was different. Unlike the Monache, they created bands of interconnected villages throughout the Owens Valley. These bands never developed a larger tribal concept or social entities, such as clans or moieties, like the Yokuts and Miwok had. Rather, they honored individuality and the family unit, as the Tubatulabal and Monache did. They even had differences of dialect within the Owens Valley area.

Settlement in the Owens Valley began more than 10,000 years ago. This was during a time when the Owens Valley was a prime location. Waters from the melting glaciers of the most recent ice age still lingered in vast Great Basin grasslands and lakes of what now are desert valleys and playas. With a total area of around 3,300 square miles, the long meadowlands of the Owens River were large enough to carry a sizable human population at elevations between 3,600 feet on the valley floor and 5,000 feet or so along the alluvial and volcanic mountain slopes.[8]

The soil of the eastern Sierra lowlands was loose granitic gravel often mixed with porous volcanic dirt or rich alluvial deposits. "Wherever water touches it, [the valley land] produces abundantly," Capt. J. W. Davidson reported in 1859, during one of the first American expeditions into the Owens Valley. "The grasses were of luxuriant growth. In one meadow . . . the grass (over two feet in height, broad leaved and juicy) extended for miles."[9]

Several different vegetation zones furnished an abundance of additional resources. The coniferous forests that reached down steep Sierra canyons provided wood, herbs, deer, and mountain sheep. By 4000 BC, piñon and juniper forests had advanced into the western Great Basin at elevations below 8,000 feet, producing pine nuts and attracting deer and antelope. In the sagebrush lands around 5,000 to 6,000 feet in elevation, rabbit, a staple, proliferated,

Piñon forests were crucial food sources for the Paiute people. —From author's files

while in lower valley wetlands and meadows, grasses, roots, tubers, and waterfowl thrived. Sierra streams furnished a good supply of mountain trout, and the Owens River contained what seemed an endless supply of the tiny, now endangered pupfish. Nearby, the Owens Lake basin contained 160 million tons of various salts washed down from the High Sierra during the ice ages, creating a perfect habitat for the brine fly larva.

In addition to the kutsavi and pe'-ag'gie, other Owens Valley foods included crickets, grasshoppers, beetles, and ants. They also gathered salt from the alkali flats south of Big Pine Lake and in the Saline Valley in the eastern desert, forming the salt into balls or cakes for family use and for trade. They traveled into the desert at least as far as the Death Valley area to harvest mesquite beans, which they ground into flour and stored for lean years. Because the weather patterns and growing seasons were so unpredictable in the rain shadow of the Sierra, the Owens Valley Paiute maintained extensive food storage systems.

During several drought periods between 6,400 and 2,900 years ago, people believed to be the direct ancestors of the Great Basin Paiutes migrated northward from southeastern California into the Owens Valley and assimilated with the earlier settlers. Just as the Penutians brought a new language, technology, and traditions to the Hokans on the west side of the Sierra, so these southern people introduced the Numic-Shoshonean language, the bow and arrow, petroglyph art, pottery, and pine-nut harvesting to the people on the east side of the range.

Most of the Owens Valley Paiute villages were on the west side of the valley along the Sierra escarpment. They sat on knolls where they were protected from winter winds but had cooling breezes in summer, and where Sierra-fed springs and rivers flowed nearby. It was a landscape dominated by expanses of sagebrush steppe, lakes, and marshes, around which game animals congregated. The semipermanent villages were composed of individual family units that contained anywhere from two to twenty people. The population density of each village's hunting and gathering area became regulated by the quantity of food available, so a land-use pattern evolved that remained largely the same for 7,000 years or more.

Before Euro-Americans arrived, an estimated 2,000 Indians lived in thirty villages throughout the Owens Valley and its east-side Sierra foothills. These villages were united into several land-utilization districts, each with communal hunting and seed rights, political unity, and a relatively rigid concept of ownership. The territory of each group of villages was jealously guarded, for resources were limited by mountain and desert landscapes beyond the confines of the lush valley.

Somewhat isolated by the High Sierra barrier on the west and surrounding deserts to the north, east, and south, the Owens Valley Paiute learned to assimilate and invent systems that worked for them in their particular environment. They managed their highly defined hunting, fishing, and gathering territories as private lands regulated by each user band, with separate communal piñon territories for harvesting the nuts. Outsiders were sometimes granted permission to gather nuts but—especially in lean years—they were generally excluded. Rather than retreating to lower elevations in winter as most tribes did, in good piñon years the Owens Valley people sometimes moved higher into the Sierra and desert mountains in order to protect and take full advantage of this primary food resource.

Trespassing by another band usually brought swift reprisal. Although wars were uncommon and the bands lived together in relative peace, squabbles did occur and territorial encroachment by foreign tribes generated several battles. This gained the Owens Valley Paiute a dubious reputation as a warring people. They so intimidated the west-side tribes with their territorial boundaries that the Yokuts often used the Western Monache as trading middlemen in order to avoid direct contact with the Paiute.

It was a reputation that told little of the Paiute way of life for, as with their neighbors the Western Monache and Tubatulabal, cooperation was essential for survival. "I learn from them that they have never been at war with any other tribe," Capt. J. W. Davidson wrote of the Owens Valley Paiute in 1859. "This would seem to be established also by their mode of Government, for they have no principal chief or leader, which warfare would render necessary, but they are ruled by the heads of families."[11]

IN ADDITION TO HARVESTING WHAT NATURE PROVIDED, the Owens Valley people eventually learned how to nurture and enhance the environment by seeding fields, pruning plants, and damming streams to divert the water flow. By around AD 1000 they had built a large irrigation system of canals flowing from Owens River tributaries in order to water large fields of their favored bulbs and tubers.[12] Most favored was the tupusi, or taboose grass, the yellow nut-grass whose roots had small, firm, sweet-tasting tubers that, when roasted, resembled miniature yams. Another favorite was nahavita, a wild hyacinth with blue, lily-shaped flowers and edible onionlike root bulbs.[13]

One of the most favored positions in an irrigation district was that of the tuvaiju, or head irrigator, who was elected each spring. A tuvaiju was required to be honest, industrious, generous, kindly, and infused with the special spirit powers of good decisions and good fortune. If the tuvaiju proved worthy, he or she could be reelected for many years. It was not the irrigator, however, but the poganabi, the village headman, who directed most of the agricultural activities.

When the poganabi announced it was time to irrigate, the tuvaiju assembled all available men to dam a main stream with boulders, brush, and sticks in order to divert the water into a large canal. After the water was drained from the stream, the people of the district villages gathered the fish left stranded in the dry bed. The head irrigator had sole responsibility for the upkeep of the dam, canal, and smaller ditches, including manipulating the mud, sod, and brush embankments with an eight-foot-long pole called a pavodo, to ensure an even water flow.

At the end of the summer, when fall winds began to blow, the tuvaiju advised the headman to gather the men to break the dam and let the waters flow back into the creek. Once again, fish were recovered—from the emptied

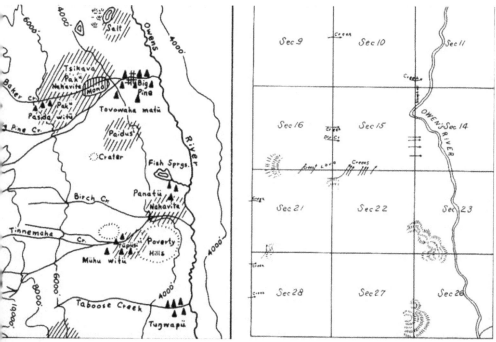

Two Owens Valley irrigation areas as drawn by J. H. Steward, 1933, and A. W. Von Schmidt, 1856. Steward's are shown as hatched areas; Von Schmidt's, of the Tinnemaha Creek area, shows canals as arrows. —From H. W. Lawton et. al., "Agriculture Among the Paiute of Owens Valley"

irrigation ditches this time—and the fields were allowed to dry so the women could harvest the plants. In addition to directing the crop cultivation, the village headman decided when the crops were ready for harvesting, allocated the amounts of produce to be given to each family, and decided how much would be communally stored for winter. If it had been a good year, he determined which unirrigated areas of rice grass and wild rye would be opened to other communities, including the neighboring Shoshone. It was the headman who made certain that not all tubers and seeds were harvested, but that the women turned some bulbs back over into the soil with digging sticks, and that some of the seeds were scattered in canal overflow areas.

Even with irrigation, however, a successful crop depended on rainfall. A general drought period occurred 800 to 150 years ago, and the manufacture of rain became of prime importance. Numic rain shamans were hired from the Coso Range east of the Sierra Nevada, for shamans from that area were believed to have special rain-making powers.

In good years, extra food could be traded. Trade was an integral part of the Paiute economy. Villages used both ancient trails and new ones they developed to connect with Western Monache and Tubatulabal trails that led to common trading grounds. By far the greatest amount of prehistoric trade in the southern Sierra Nevada took place across the highest part of the range. The Mono Trail to Yosemite became a primary route.

TRADING AND INTERMARRYING WITH THE MIWOK, Western Monache, Tubatulabal, Shoshone, and occasionally even the Yokuts, the Owens Valley Paiute adopted whatever technology, inventions, and social customs might serve them. Their bark mountain dwellings were like Western Monache and Miwok shelters, but their valley residences—called tonis—were dome- or cone-shaped and grass- or brush-covered, much like those of the Kern River Tubatulabal. They practiced abortion as the Tubatulabal did. They irrigated fields but planted none of the maize that the Southern Paiute Panamint tribes in the Coso Range and Little Lake areas did; they pruned and burned their tobacco fields, but did not sow the plants as the nearby Kawaiisu and Coso tribes did.

Like all their neighbors, the Owens Valley people enjoyed a fall gathering of feasting, gambling, and dancing, but with songs and games uniquely their own. They differed from other Sierra peoples in some of their funeral practices: they buried their dead rather than cremating them and held mourning ceremonies

Remnants of rush-covered Owens Valley tonis —Courtesy Inyo National Forest archives

in the spring rather than fall. Their puberty rites followed the intricacies of the desert tribes, but they seldom drank jimson weed concoctions.

Women were counted on to care for those in need. Not only did women take care of their own households and children, they were also expected to contribute to the health and welfare of the larger community. As she grew older, a woman took on much of the care of her grandchildren. She often made a basketry cradle for each new grandchild's arrival, carefully designing a zigzag pattern on the hood for a girl and inclined dashes for a boy. She helped feed, clothe, entertain, and instruct each new generation as they grew, just as her grandparents had done for her.

Like the Western Monache, Owens Valley women wove baskets, but they developed their own weaves and twining. They also learned pottery-making

and developed it to an artistry beyond that of other Sierra tribes. Only a few women produced the pottery, for it was considered a special art form. Reddish brown clay was obtained from preferred local sites, one of them near the village of Fish Springs. The women ground and sifted this clay and mixed it with water tempered with decomposed granite collected from Baker Creek.

Owens Valley brownware was special pottery valued for both its practicality and its beauty.
—Courtesy Eastern California Museum

Next, they gathered desert mallow—abundant along Big Pine Creek—boiled it into thick syrup, and mixed it with the clay. They shaped the pots by hand, with a clay pancake forming the base and long, narrow strips pressed onto the base to form the sides. The pots were smoothed with fingers dipped in the mallow syrup, then etched with decorative designs. Finally, they dried the vessels and fired them in sagebrush coals. The craftsmanship and beauty of the Owens Valley brownware made it an important trade item.

Another art form practiced by the Paiute, as well as most prehistoric people, was rock art. The earliest types, dating from 5500 to 500 BC, were pit-and-groove style, in which the artists chipped small pits into the surfaces of boulders. Dating from 1000 BC to AD 1500 or 1600, came a pecked style

Petroglyphs—pecked and scratched figures in rock—date as early as 7,000 years ago. Many in the Owens Valley region depict hunting figures. —Courtesy Inyo National Forest archives

that was common in the Great Basin and especially in the Owens Valley.[14] It entailed pecking images into the rock in shapes of circles, circle chains, sun disks, meanders, wavy lines, star figures, dots, rectangular grids, bird tracks, rakes, and cross-hatching. The images in the Owens Valley Paiute area were highly abstract, in contrast to their eastern Shoshonean neighbors' work in the Coso Range; the Coso pictures were representational, with stylized anthropomorphic figures, sometimes larger than life.

Following the pecked style of petroglyphs was a scratched or incised style, in which the artist cut lines into the boulders with a sharp rock in a single stroke. The images consisted of straight lines, sun figures, and cross-hatching often placed over other figures, perhaps indicating attempts of later Numic peoples to obliterate the earlier designs. No one knows with certainty the intent or purpose of rock art. "Innumerable attempts have been made to ascertain the meanings of petroglyphs and pictographs from Indians living at present in the regions where they occur," Julian Steward wrote in 1929. "They have invariably met with failure. The Indians disclaim all knowledge of their meaning or origin."[15]

In spite of Steward's assessment, many indigenous people of the Great Basin and Sierra Nevada regions related several meanings of the rock art to early white settlers. They connected them to hunting and puberty rituals and to shamanistic powers. Many rock images, especially petroglyphs in the southern Sierra region, appear to be connected with hunting activities. Maps of game trails, when compared with maps of petroglyph locations, have shown that in many instances the rock art is located along the trails or in winter grazing areas. "They are not aimless 'doodling', nor are they deliberate and planned expressions of the artistic impulse," Heizer and Baumhoff concluded in 1962.[16] There also are indications that some rock art occurred at camping sites, trail junctions, water holes, creeks, and springs. Petroglyphs near sites of permanent prehistoric villages have also been found in the Owens Valley, above Bishop and at Fish Springs.

OWENS VALLEY PAIUTE STORIES AND MYTHS were much like those of Southern California and Great Basin tribes, but with their own variations and styles. Some tales related to events deep in the past, such as a time of great ice in the mountains when the weather was so cold that all trade and hunting in the highlands had to stop. Others told of a great drought, when the stored food was exhausted and many people died; of a time when there were no piñon forests, when great animals roamed the land, and hunting them was the main means of survival; of the days when there was no irrigation, no pottery, no bow and arrow, no mortar and pestle, and the people spoke a different language.

Some stories reached even further back, to the myths of the ancients and animal people; of great waters to the east, south and west, and of people who lived far across them; of a time when the entire desert was a land of green meadows, tall trees, great lakes, and plentiful game; a time before volcanoes burned the land and turned it into desert.

Stories told to children were based in the present and contained strong morals. One was of Nunumic, the great cannibal giant whose long tongue could reach through the doors of bad people's tonis and, with one sweep, pull all the people out and eat them up. Another warned children to be home by nightfall or a giant woman wearing a basket cap lined with fish hooks would clap it on their heads, drag them up the side of the crater above Tuniga Witu (Fish Springs), and throw them into it.[17] And if they didn't believe it, all they had to do was look at the gully in the side of the crater—it had been formed by children being dragged up there.

Several cottontail stories cautioned children about the folly of trying to be something they weren't. Others instructed them in ways to relate to nature. If someone pointed at a new moon or at a rainbow, his finger would get sore or even drop off. Orion was the net of a rabbit drive, and its position told how far the night had passed. The Pleiades were men racing home from the cottontail hunt. The North Star stood in water without moving. Falling stars could bring sickness or death, shooting evil into a person just as bad shamans did. Tiwap, the universe, was a dome over the earth, which was held in the hand of a creature that shook when he moved, causing earthquakes.

The moon was an omen of weather patterns. Some said its eclipse was its death, and its return was the reemergence of life. The lunar phases were watched carefully, for when it was a crescent on its back there would be storms coming, and when it was on its end the weather would be dry. The color and size of auras that sometimes surrounded the sun and moon indicated the degrees of storm and cold. Flying cobwebs in the air were indicators of a storm the next day, and each breeze might be an *osojapu*, the spirits' breath that foretold a storm. The winds and the varying angles of the sun told when each of the five seasons—fall, winter, spring, summer, and midsummer—had arrived.

Time was a never-ending cycle that always followed the sun, yet was never the same. It was the flow of events: building dams and tearing them down; pine nuts ripening; deer migrating down to their winter feeding grounds; the first thunderstorm of spring; a devastating flood on Oak Creek; the incursion of a family of Panamint Shoshone on Magpie Creek; mad dances and tribal disputes; marriages and births; accidents, illnesses, and deaths.

The seasons were distinct on the east side of the Sierra Nevada. Summers were long, heated by the surrounding deserts but often cooled by mountain-generated thunderstorms. Autumns were crisp, sun-filled, and pleasant. Winters were often cold, with bitter winds sweeping down from the high Sierra peaks.

Springs were always the most difficult, for the warmer days seemed reluctant to settle in. Winter often returned long after the paper birch trees that lined the creeks had leafed out; after the willows were budding and the evening primrose was showing green; sometimes even two moon cycles after blue, yellow, and white flowers had dared to blossom between the warm crevices of volcanic rock. Day after day, sometimes into June, wind clouds strung themselves in long waves across the high crest of the Sierra Nevada, drawing a curtain of snow across each canyon. To the east, against the desert ranges, billowing clouds dropped snow on the winter piñon camps. A brisk wind reached down from the Sierra to the villages, making people retreat to their tonis for warmth. Often, unaccustomed to staying indoors, they would emerge again, wrapped in rabbit-skin blankets, to sit in the morning sunshine.

FOR AN OLD SHAMAN, a long winter seemed a portent that his time was growing short. Since his first spirit dream as a very young boy, a shaman lived in fear of his end, an end that often was violent.

While most boys and girls had dreams of their animal-spirit helpers who could be called on for assistance, a future shaman had recurring dreams, often beginning at age five or six, that told him he must become a *puhaga*, or spirit doctor. It was a calling he could not deny, whether he wanted it or not. He would tell no one of the dreams, except his father or another relative who already was a puhaga who could train him. His early training was mostly learning how to

A Paiute shaman —Courtesy Bureau of Land Management, Inyo files

always be good so he could not be turned into an evil shaman. By the time he reached puberty, he would have memorized several spirit songs, sung to him in his dreams by his personal animal spirit. These were the source of his healing powers, and he sang them, alone, until they were a part of him.

As he approached manhood, between the ages of fourteen and nineteen, his father and the village headman might send him on a long journey. If he chose to go, he would set out to discover the larger world in the company of several other promising boys training to become shamans or headmen. It was an important journey, for leadership recognition was often based on a man's travel experience and connections.

Equipped only with bows and arrows and a few simple tools, bands of select young men roamed the desert lands for periods ranging from several months to as long as five years. They stopped at foreign villages to the south and east, from Arizona up to Idaho and from California to Utah, to learn the customs and life ways of other peoples. They saw tribes that planted corn, squash, beans, and melons in the desert sands beside large rivers. They observed irrigation systems much like those in the Owens Valley. In the south, they visited tribes that lived in clay and mud dwellings, and in the north, discovered homes constructed of hides and rough-hewn boards. They traded for cloth made of cotton rather than of tule; joined in differing dances and games; watched intricate puberty rites; and heard countless variations of the myths and stories on which they had been weaned as children. They learned of diverse social structures, moieties, and totems, and observed the practices of various shamans.

When the young men returned home, they were expected to marry and take their positions in the community. For the shaman in training, this meant learning the ways of the spirit doctor, for if he did not, his special powers might turn to evil and his family could come to harm. He spent many years apprenticed to an older shaman. If he was to be a healing shaman, he spent his summers collecting healing plants and developing them into medicines. He practiced the songs and dances that his dream spirits continued to show him. He learned how to suck out poisons and evil from those who had been injected with them by bad doctors and witches.

For all his studies, he still had to wait until the spirits called him in a special dream before he could become a full shaman in his own right. Sometimes that did not happen until he was nearly middle aged. In the meantime, he spent his energies working toward perfection, for he knew if he let bad thoughts enter him or if he did not perform his healings carefully, evil would come and make him a bad doctor. He lived in constant fear of losing his healing powers. There was no room for mistakes, not only in the doctoring, but in his daily activities, too. Until he achieved his full status, he was expected to participate fully in community affairs—sitting in council, joining hunts and battles, helping to maintain the district's irrigation systems, and performing whatever other work needed to be done.

After a man became a shaman, his wife's duties and responsibilities increased significantly. In her own way, she was a missionary, spreading the word of her husband's talents and helping to create belief in his powers. She was expected to learn the different dialects of the Owens Valley and surrounding territories so as to gain the confidence of every village. She also acted as helpmate and advisor to her husband, going with him to lend assistance during long healing sessions and comforting the family of the patient. She traveled widely with her husband on his calls and on trips into the Sierra highlands to collect medicinal herbs.

In everything she did, the shaman's wife asked the spirits to help her, her husband, and her family. She knew that all things—plants, rocks, water, sun, stars, moon, and wind—understood what she said, but the spirits did not always help. Eventually, a healing shaman almost always ran into trouble. A jealous or evil fellow shaman might shoot his patients with illness or take away his powers. If his healing efforts failed, the patient's family or even the whole community might decide he had become evil, especially if someone of importance died. A shaman accused of killing someone was usually put to death.

However death came, the shaman would most likely be forewarned. If a whirlwind approached him, the ghost of his own father could be in it, calling the shaman's soul to join him. To dream of the dead was a bad omen. Even worse was to dream of the evil owl.

A shaman warned of his impending death often stored his wealth and doctoring implements in one of Owens Valley's volcanic caves, placing forked willow spirit sticks in front of the cave, which would forever prevent all but his family from entering it. The exact moment of his death probably came unexpectedly. A victim's family member might attack him or hire someone to do it, sometimes in an ambush or a nighttime assault. Some doomed shamans fled from the valley, but others did nothing to resist their fate, certain it was justice for their failure.

A disgraced shaman's body was not buried but burned with his personal possessions to destroy the evil spirits that had come to reside in him. His family gathered the ashes and covered them over with a small mound of dirt. At the mourning ceremony and cry dance the following spring, his wife would smooth the mound flat and seed it to hide all traces of the gravesite. As she covered the ashes, she might ask her husband to go away and not to haunt her or visit the village people in their dreams. She never spoke his name again, lest his soul think she had called him and come back to serve evil witches.

After the mourning ceremony, the shaman's widow gathered her own belongings and took them to another toni in her village to live out the rest of her days. As she awaited her own death, she could not know that the end was also coming for the cultures of all the Sierra's prehistoric people.

Epilogue

THE BIRD AND ANIMAL PEOPLE LEAVE
A Wukchumni Yokuts Tale

One day, the ancient animal people on the Kaweah River had a feast and meeting in which they talked about a change that was going to take place. "Now," said Wee-hay'-sit, the Mountain Lion, "We will let Tro'-khud, the Eagle, talk first. We will see what he says we must do about these new kind of people who are coming."

Tro'-khud said, "Now all of us bird and animal people must go away. We must find a new place for each of us to live. We all have to make our living differently, too. They are going to live here in this country where we have been living. We must go away. They will live in our villages. They are going to live differently from us. The men are going to kill Hoey, the Deer, and use his skin to make many things. The women are going to make baskets and cook and work, making acorn bread. We will call them Mi'-eh, the Indians.

"I am going to tell all of you people what you are going to do when these new people are here," he continued. "Some of you people have been eating meat and we are going to send you to live where you cannot bother Mi'-eh, the Indians, who are coming soon.

167

Wee-hay'-sit, the Mountain Lion, is the second headman here. He will take charge now. Well, Wee-hay'-sit, what am I going to do when these new people come?"

"Well, you had better be Tro'-khud, the big Bald Eagle," the Mountain Lion said.

"What am I going to eat?" the Eagle asked.

"You are going to eat young deer or any kind of good meat," he replied, then he asked, "Who is the next one?"

Ki'-yoo, the Coyote, wanted to be Eagle, too, so he could fly around. But Tro'-khud told him to sit down and keep quiet. He told Condor he must stay in the high rocks and eat anything he found along the hills. "We must hurry now, because it is almost time for us

"Now all of us bird and animal people must go away. We must find a new place for each of us to live." —From C. Hart Merriam, *The Dawn of the World*, courtesy Bancroft Library, UC Berkeley

to make the Indians," he said, and he asked Kah'-cha Choo'-wuh, the Lizard, to name all the other bird and animal people and tell them where to live.

Lizard told Blue Jay to plant all of the oak trees to grow acorns for the new people. He told Deer that he was going to be good meat for these new people. "They are going to kill you all the time," he told Hoey, "but as soon as they kill you, you leave your meat for them and go away and live again."

Next came Antelope, Elk, Mountain Sheep, Dove, Pigeon, and Quail. "You will all be good meat, too. The Indians will kill you, but you will have to stay dead. You will not be able to live again."

Tro'-khud called all of the fish: the Lake Trout, Salmon, Sturgeon, and all of the rest. "You people must live in the rivers and lakes," Lizard told them. "You can never go on land again. The Indians will catch and eat you. No-ho'-o, the Black Bear, you are to live in the mountains. Sometimes you can eat the jimson weed root. You will be the only animal to eat it."

The Wolf was to stay on the plains and in the hills and eat squirrels and rabbits and antelope, but never bother the Indians. The Hawk must eat the Squirrel, maybe the Quail, and anything new that came along. The Wild Cat must live in the rocks and catch small things to eat and not bother the new people who were coming.

Lizard told each of them what he was to do, until only the Coyote was left. "You are Ki'-yoo," Lizard told him. "You are to run around the hills and eat the Squirrel."

And so Lizard named all of them and sent them away to their new homes.

—Adapted from Frank F. Latta, *California Indian Folklore*.[1]

FOR THOUSANDS OF YEARS, California's prehistoric people lived on the land, sharing it with the wild creatures. So many generations had passed since the first people migrated to North America that their Asian and Nordic origins had become nothing more than myths and lingering folktales of a primeval animal people.

But a new people were about to arrive. This time there were no meetings, no supernatural powers to prepare for their coming. Still, like the old-time bird and animal people, the indigenous people of the Sierra Nevada region would have to find a new place for themselves.

The first indications of the change were rumors that passed along trails from the western sea all the way to the Sierra Nevada. Chumash fishermen had seen two sailing ships off the southern California coast. Strange men of strange dress had come ashore bearing gifts of beads. Fearful yet curious, the Chumash greeted their visitors as was their custom, exchanging gifts and food, then they watched the ships sail off again. From that day, wherever they went to hunt or trade, they informed others of the strange people they had met.

These were not the first stories about strange men arriving. From the far south came tales of wars in which every person in some villages had been killed or taken as a slave. Later, other people spoke of pale, bearded men riding on horses, making their way north from the southern desert lands. But until the Spaniard Juan Rodriguez Cabrillo landed in 1542, California people had never seen a European man.

For the next two hundred years, European ships and colonists plied California's coast. They set up military and trading outposts inland, but virtually none of the strangers approached the Sierra. By 1772 only a handful of Spanish army deserters had disappeared into the southern mountains, where they lived with the native people.

In April of 1776, the year of America's Declaration of Independence from England, Spanish missionary Francisco Garcés came to the High Sierra region from the Southwest, bringing the first modern changes. On his journey through the southern Sierra foothills, Garcés introduced metal trinkets and tools, the written word, Christianity, and the concept of modern timekeeping. A steady stream of soldiers, missionaries, fur trappers, gold seekers, and settlers followed. Within seventy-five years, the newcomers' living patterns, diseases, tools, weapons, transportation modes, and sheer numbers would impact the Sierra Nevada and its original residents in ways that thousands of years of prehistoric usage had not. The High Sierra region would never be the same.

Geologic Time Line*

Era	Period	Epoch	
CENOZOIC 65 million years ago to today	**Quaternary** 2 million years ago to today	**Holocene** 11,000 years ago to today	Sierra Nevada continues to grow. Warming period established. Large Sierra glaciers vanish. Mono Craters continue to form. Inyo Craters erupt, creating local cooling and cirque glaciers in high Sierra region
		Pleistocene 2 million to 11,000 years ago	Modern Sierra uplift continues. Volcanic episodes in Sierra create Mono Craters. Several glacial and interglacial periods occur. Bering land bridge exposed. First humans arrive in California. Larger mammals, such as mammoth, develop.
	Tertiary 65 to 2 million years ago	**Pliocene** 5 to 2 million years ago	Major uplift and tilting of modern Sierra Nevada. Owens Valley subsides. Sierra begins to move south from Klamath Range. Widespread volcanism along Sierra crest and in Great Basin. Glacial period in northern continents dries land. Sequoia forests diminish. Vegetation dominated by grasslands. Grazing mammals develop.
		Miocene 24 to 5 million years ago	Major grasslands form. Active volcanic period. Sierra batholith surfaces as granitic intrusions during series of uplifts.
		Oligocene 34 to 24 million years ago	Magmatic uprisings with mudflows fill canyons in northern ancestral Sierra. Grasses first appear. Elephants, horses, bears, follow. Coniferous forests retreat. Deserts appear.
		Eocene 55 to 34 million years ago	Large fault system occupies western continental margin. Ancestral Sierra is worn down to hilly upland Hot spell lasts for 5 to 10 million years with glacial melting. Most modern orders of mammals appear.
		Paleocene 65 to 55 million years ago	Erosion reduces ancestral Sierra highlands. Modern Sierra begins uplift. Widespread volcanism. Cooling climate initiates continental glaciations. Dinosaur extinction begins. Small and medium-size mammals dominate.

All dating is approximate, formulated from various sources.

Era		Epoch	
MESOZOIC 248 to 65 million years ago		**Cretaceous** 144 to 65 million years ago	Ancestral Sierra Nevada rises to 13,000 ft. Large amounts of magma rise and crystallize below surface to form granite core. Core separates into Sierra and Klamath Ranges. Eruptions create volcanic uplands. New California coastline forms to west. Climate warms. Broad-leafed and coniferous forests, flowering plants, insects, birds, and mammals develop.
		Jurassic 206 to 144 million years ago	Pangaea breaks apart. Atlantic Ocean spreads. North American continent starts moving west. Subduction zone returns on western margin. Ancestral Sierra begins to form. Dinosaurs roam lowlands. First birds and mammals appear.
		Triassic 248 to 206 million years ago	Pacific Plate subduction zone changes to fault system that lasts 2.5 million years. Emergence of dinosaurs.
PALEOZOIC 543 to 248 million years ago		**Permian** 290 to 248 million years ago	Massive volcanic episode. First known mass extinction of land and marine species occurs.
		Carboniferous 354 to 290 million years ago	North America collides with Europe and Africa to form Pangaea. North America and Europe, located near the equator, are covered by shallow seas. Coral reefs and sedimentary deposits develop along North America's western margin. Limestone forms. First reptiles appear.
		Devonian 417 to 354 million years ago	Tetrapods (vertebrate fish and amphibians with four appendages) evolve. Arachnids, such as spiders and scorpions, develop. Insects appear.
		Silurian 443 to 417 million years ago	Climate stabilizes. Glacial ice melts and sea level rises. Algae, fish, shell-covered animals evolve. First land plants appear.
		Ordovician 490 to 443 million years ago	Continents start to converge. Oldest known Sierra rocks form in deep sea. Marine plants and invertebrates develop.
		Cambrian 543 to 490 million years ago	Rodinia's continental rifting completed. Glaciations cover Sahara, South Africa, and Brazil. Shelled organisms appear.
PROTEROZOIC 2,500 to 543 million years ago		**Neoproterozoic** 900 to 543 million years ago	Rodinia starts to break up. Rifting creates new ocean basins with sea-floor spreading. First marine organisms appear.
		Mesoproterozoic 1,600 to 900 million years ago	Oxygen increases in atmosphere. Earth's first known ice age takes place.
		Paleoproterozoic 2,500 to 1,600 million years ago	Supercontinent Rodinia begins to form. Western North American margin established east of today's Sierra region.
ARCHAEAN		3,800 to 2,500 million years ago	Cooling of Earth's crust and initial continent formation. Oceans develop. Bacteria appear.
HADEAN		4,600 to 3,800 million years ago	Formation of solar system and Earth.

Notes and References

Introduction

1. Thomas F. Howard, *Sierra Crossing* (Berkeley: University of California Press, 1998), 15–16. The Buenaventura River was the name given today's Green River by Franciscan fathers Dominguez and Escalante in 1776.
2. Clarence King, *Mountaineering in the Sierra Nevada* (1872; reprint, Lincoln: University of Nebraska Press, 1970), 6.
3. Wallace Elliott and Company, *History of Tulare County*, California (San Francisco: Wallace W. Elliott & Co., 1883), 115. The glaciers mentioned in this quote are now gone or dying at an accelerating pace.
4. W. A. Chalfant, *The Story of Inyo* (Bishop, Calif.: Chalfant Press, 1933), 50.

Additional Sources

Francois E. Matthes, *The Incomparable Valley: A Geologic Interpretation of the Yosemite* (Berkeley: University of California Press, 1950).

James G. Moore, *Exploring the Highest Sierra* (Stanford: Stanford University Press, 2000).

University of California, SNEP Science Team, and Special Consultants, *Sierra Nevada Ecosystem Project*, 3 vols. (Davis, Calif.: Centers for Water and Wildland Resources, University of California–Davis, 1996).

1. Geology

1. The big mountain is now called Mt. Shasta.
2. Frank F. Latta, "Lim'-ik and Ahl'-wut Make the Mountains" in *California Indian Folklore* (1936; reprint, Exeter, Calif.: Bear State Books, 1999), 63–64; Stephen Powers, "Origin of the Mountains," *Tribes of California* (1877; reprint, Berkeley: University of California Press, 1976), 383–84. Variations of this story were told by the Yaulmeni Yokuts (Tubatulabal) of Kern River, the Western Monos of Kings River, and the Chuckchansi Yokuts of the Tule River. Many folktales appear with variations among several of the Sierra groups.
3. All geological dating in this book is generalized and subject to interpretation. Geologic time tables are classified by periods rather than by dates. As those classifications mean little to the student of history, I have attempted throughout this book to place geologic occurrences into a very general time frame, based on various geological sources. Bear in mind that the facts are subject to continuing debate, as dating theories vary greatly among geologists.

Additional Sources

David D. Alt and Donald W. Hyndman, *Roadside Geology of Northern and Central California* (Missoula, Mont.: Mountain Press Publishing, 2000).

Paul C. Bateman, "Geologic Structure and History of the Sierra Nevada," in *UMR* (University of Missouri–Rolla) *Journal* 1 (April 1968).

Martin H. P. Bott, *The Interior of the Earth: Its Structure, Constitution and Evolution* (New York: Elsevier Science Publishing, 1982).

Joel Despain, *Hidden Beneath the Mountains* (Dayton, Ohio: Cave Books, 2003).

Susan Elizabeth Hough, *Finding Fault in California* (Missoula, Mont.: Mountain Press Publishing, 2004).

Craig Jones, Jeffrey R. Unruh, and Leslie J. Sancher, "The Role of Gravitational Potential Energy in the Active Deformation in the Southwestern United States," in *Nature* 381, no. 6577 (May 2, 1996).

Ted Konigsmark, *Geologic Trips: Sierra Nevada* (Gualala, Calif.: GeoPress, 2002).

James G. Moore, *Exploring the Highest Sierra* (Stanford: Stanford University Press, 2000).

David Perlman, "Molten Rock May Hold Key to Rise of High Sierra," in *San Francisco Chronicle*, July 30, 2004.

Frank Press and Raymond Siever, *Understanding Earth* (New York: W. H. Freeman & Co., 1994).

David Ritchie, *Superquake! Why Earthquakes Occur and When the Big One Will Hit Southern California* (New York: Crown Publishers, 1988).

Jason B. Saleeby, "On Some Aspects of the Geology of the Sierra Nevada," in *Classic Cordilleran Concepts: A View from California*, Special Paper 338 (Boulder, Colo.: Geological Society of America, 1999).

Jack R. Sheehan, "Tectonic Overview of Owens Valley Region," in *Guidebook to the Eastern Sierra Nevada, Owens Valley, White-Inyo Range* (Los Angeles: University of California–Los Angeles, Department of Earth and Space Sciences, 1980).

Tracy I. Storer and Robert L. Usinger, *Sierra Nevada Natural History* (Berkeley: University of California Press, 1963).

Brian Wernicke et al., "Origin of High Mountains in the Continents: The Southern Sierra Nevada," in *Science* 271 (January 12, 1996).

2. Climate

1.   W. A. Chalfant, *The Story of Inyo* (Bishop, Calif.: Chalfant Press, 1933), 68.

Additional Sources

David D. Alt and Donald W. Hyndman, *Roadside Geology of Northern and Central California* (Missoula, Mont.: Mountain Press Publishing, 2000).

Elizabeth L. Horn, *Sierra Nevada Wildflowers* (Missoula, Mont.: Mountain Press Publishing, 1998).

McClatchy Tribune, "Ancient Hot Spell May Hold Clues to Warming," in *Visalia Times Delta*, August 26 and 27, 2006.

James G. Moore, *Exploring the Highest Sierra* (Stanford: Stanford University Press, 2000).

Paleontology Research Group, Dept. of Geology, *Paleofiles* (2006), www.bristol.ac.uk.

Frank Press and Raymond Siever, *Understanding Earth* (New York: W. H. Freeman & Co., 1994).

Allan A. Schoenherr, *A Natural History of California* (Berkeley: University of California Press, 1992).

Carl K. Seyfert and Leslie A. Sirkin, *Earth History and Plate Tectonics: An Introduction to Historical Geology* (New York: Harper & Row, 1973).

Tracy I. Storer and Robert L. Usinger, *Sierra Nevada Natural History* (Berkeley: University of California Press, 1963).

Don and Maureen Tarling, *Continental Drift: A Study of the Earth's Moving Surface* (Garden City, N.Y.: Doubleday & Co., 1971).
University of California, SNEP Science Team, and Special Consultants, *Sierra Nevada Ecosystem Project*, 3 vols. (Davis, Calif.: Centers for Water and Wildland Resources, University of California–Davis, 1996).
Kim West, *Extinction: Cycles of Life and Death Through Time*, 1996. Hooper Virtual Paleontological Museum, hoopermuseum.earthsci.carleton.ca//extinction/extincmenu.html.

3. Vegetation

1. Ow-wah-ne is the Paiute name for old Mt. Tom.
2. W. A. Chalfant, "Owens Valley Legend of Creation," in *The Story of Inyo* (Bishop, Calif.: Chalfant Press, 1933), 53–55.
3. John Muir, "Peaks and Glaciers of the High Sierra," in Muir, ed., *West of the Rocky Mountains* (reprint, Philadelphia: Running Press, 1976), 2.
4. Ibid., 7.

Additional Sources

David Dulitz, "Mountain Home State Forest," report of Mounain Home State Park field trip, August 2007, in *Tulare County Historical Society Newsletter* 239 (December 2007).
Verna R. Johnston, *Sierra Nevada: The Naturalist's America* (Boston: Houghton Mifflin, 1970).
James G. Moore, *Exploring the Highest Sierra* (Stanford: Stanford University Press, 2000).
Jim Paruk, *Sierra Nevada Tree Identifier* (Yosemite, Calif.: Yosemite Natural History Association, 1997).
Roderick Peattie, ed., *The Sierra Nevada: Range of Light* (New York: Vanguard Press, 1947).
Raymond D. Ratliff, *Meadows in the Sierra Nevada of California: State of Knowledge*, General Technical Report PSW-84, U.S. Department of Agriculture, Forest Service (Berkeley, Calif.: Pacific Southwest Forest and Range Experiment Station, 1985).
Allan A. Schoenherr, *A Natural History of California* (Berkeley: University of California Press, 1992).
James Clifford Shirley, *The Redwoods of Coast and Sierra* (Berkeley: University of California Press, 1940).
John H. Skinner, "Placer Big Trees," in *Sierra Heritage*, May–June 2005.
Tracy I. Storer and Robert L. Usinger, *Sierra Nevada Natural History* (Berkeley: University of California Press, 1963).
University of California, SNEP Science Team, and Special Consultants, *Sierra Nevada Ecosystem Project*, 3 vols. (Davis, Calif.: Centers for Water and Wildland Resources, University of California–Davis, 1996).
Stephen Whitney, *Sierra Club Naturalists' Guide to the Sierra Nevada* (San Francisco: Sierra Club Books, 1979).

4. Animals

1. "The Indian tribes of [the Sierra region] have a tradition of a time when the desert waste was covered with water and the people inhabited only the highest peaks." From Frank F. Latta, "Saga of Rancho El Tejon," in *Memorial and Biographical History* (Bakersfield, Calif.: Bear State Books, 1976), 20.
2. Frank F. Latta, "How the Wuk-chum'-nee World Was Made" and "The Yowl-may'-nee World" in *California Indian Folklore* (1936; reprint, Exeter, Calif.: Bear State Books, 1999), 13–15, 19–20.
3. The Sierra Nevada region was evidently under oceanic waters for at least 500 million years. During the last 250 million years it was under a shallow sea abundant with marine life.
4. Dinosaurs were alive on earth for approximately 150 million years, beginning in the Triassic period, 248 to 206 million years ago. Today, there is considerable discussion regarding the length of time it took for their total extinction.

Additional Sources

W. W. Jameson, Jr., and Hans J. Peeters, *California Mammals* (Berkeley: University of California Press, 1988).

James G. Moore, *Exploring the Highest Sierra* (Stanford: Stanford University Press, 2000).

New York Times, "Study: Mass Extinction Didn't Give Rise to Mammals," in *Nature*, March 29, 2007.

C. Kristina Roper and David M. Graber, "Competition and Niche Overlap between Native Americans and Grizzly Bears on the Western Slope of the Sierra Nevada," undated manuscript, Sequoia National Park archives, Three Rivers, Calif.

Allan A. Schoenherr, *A Natural History of California* (Berkeley: University of California Press, 1992).

Tracy I. Storer and Robert L. Usinger, *Sierra Nevada Natural History* (Berkeley: University of California Press, 1963).

Lowell Sumner and Joseph F. Dixon, *Birds and Mammals of the Sierra Nevada* (Berkeley: University of California Press, 1953).

University of California, SNEP Science Team, and Special Consultants, *Sierra Nevada Ecosystem Project*, 3 vols. (Davis, Calif.: Centers for Water and Wildland Resources, University of California–Davis, 1996).

Stephen Whitney, *Sierra Club Naturalists' Guide to the Sierra Nevada* (San Francisco: Sierra Club Books, 1979).

5. Human Settlement

1. Stephen Powers, "The Creation of Man," in *Tribes of California* (1877; reprint, Berkeley: University of California Press, 1976), 358–60.
2. Albert B. Elsasser, *The Archaeology of the Sierra Nevada in California and Nevada* (Berkeley: University of California Press, 1960), 26.

Additional Sources

Galen Clark, *Indians of the Yosemite Valley and Vicinity* (Yosemite, Calif.: Galen Clark, 1907).

Joe Doctor, "California Yokuts Indian Language Traced to Siberi," in *Sun, Herald, Echo*, December 26, 1984.

Anna H. Gayton, *Yokuts and Western Mono Ethnography: Tulare Lake, Southern Valley, and Central Foothill Yokuts*, University of California Publications in Anthropological Records, vol. 10, bk. 1 (Berkeley: University of California Press, 1948).

Susan K. Goldberg, "Cultural Resources Investigations for Proposed Amendment to the Haas-Kings River Project Application (FERC 1988)," commissioned report by Infotec Research, Sonora, Calif., for Pacific Gas & Electric Company, 1986, Pacific Gas & Electric Company archives, San Francisco, Calif.

Robert F. Heizer and Albert B. Elsasser, *The Natural World of the California Indians* (Berkeley: University of California Press, 1980).

Conrad Phillip Kottak, *Anthropology: The Exploration of Human Diversity*, 2nd ed. (New York: Random House, 1978).

Charles C. Mann, "America's Pristine Myth," in *Christian Science Monitor*, September 1, 2005.

Michael J. Moratto, *California Archaeology* (Orlando: Academic Press, 1984).

Carl K. Seyfert and Leslie A. Sirkin, *Earth History and Plate Tectonics: An Introduction to Historical Geology* (New York: Harper & Row, 1973).

Peter N. Spotts, "When Humans First Came to the Americas," in *Christian Science Monitor*, n.d., 2008.

Nathan Stevens, "Prehistoric Use of the Alpine Sierra Nevada," master's thesis, California State University–Sacramento, 2002.

University of California, SNEP Science Team, and Special Consultants, *Sierra Nevada Ecosystem Project*, 3 vols. (Davis, Calif.: Centers for Water and Wildland Resources, University of California–Davis, 1996).

Otto J. Von Sadovsky, "The Discovery of California: Breaking the Silence of the Siberia-to-America Migrators," in *The Californians* 2, no. 6 (November– December 1984).

Elva Younkin, ed., *Coso Rock Art: A New Perspective* (Ridgecrest, Calif.: Maturango Press, 1998).

6. The Tubatulabal

1. Erminie W. Voegelin, "Myth of Contest to Determine Division of Labor" in *Tubatulabal Ethnography* (Berkeley: University of California Press, 1938), 53–55.

2. Ibid., 1. In most indigenous Sierra communities, the people say they have lived in the area "always."

3. The names of the various subgroups have been spelled and pronounced in many ways by other indigenous groups, early explorers, settlers, archaeologists, and ethnologists. The names and spellings presented here are the most widely used today.

4. Edward W. Gifford, *Tubatulabal and Kawaiisu Kinship Terms* (Berkeley: University of California Press, 1917), 222.

5. Voegelin, *Tubatulabal Ethnography*, 43. "Sometimes no money [was] paid for a woman. [The] man obtained the woman's parents' consent to marry their daughter, then he and [the] woman lived with [the] woman's parents for a year or so, [the] man helping his wife's parents during this time."

6. Ibid., 46.

7.   None of the Sierra Nevada Indians practiced organized religion as Euro-
      Americans define it. Formal religion and worship arrived with the Spanish
      missionaries. Indian stories with references to God reflect the influence of white
      culture.

Additional Sources

Author interview with William Horst, Porterville, Calif., October 9, 1993.

James C. Bard et al., "Kennedy Meadows Cultural Resources Data Recovery Project,"
      typescript report prepared by Kobari Environmental Management Corp.,
      Hayward, Calif., for U.S. Department of Agriculture, Sequoia National Forest,
      1985, Sequoia National Forest archives, Porterville, Calif.

Bret Bradigan, "Kern River Valley Indian Community: A Historical Overview,
      Prehistory to 1863," series of articles in *Kern Valley Sun*, Kernville, Calif., n.d.

Eugene Burmeister, *Early Days in Kern* (Bakersfield, Calif.: Cardon House, 1963).

Galen Clark, *Indians of the Yosemite Valley and Vicinity* (Yosemite, Calif.: Galen
      Clark, 1907).

Harold E. Driver, *Culture Element Distributions 6: Southern Sierra Nevada*, University
      of California Publications in Anthropological Records, vol. 1, bk. 2 (Berkeley:
      University of California Press, 1937).

Anna H. Gayton, *Yokuts and Western Mono Ethnography: Tulare Lake, Southern
      Valley, and Central Foothill Yokuts*, University of California Publications in
      Anthropological Records, vol. 10, bk. 1 (Berkeley: University of California Press,
      1948).

Robert F. Heizer, ed., *Handbook of North American Indians* (Washington, D.C.:
      Smithsonian Institution, 1978).

A. L. Kroeber, *Handbook of the Indians of California* (reprint, New York: Dover
      Publications, 1976).

Annie Mitchell, *The Way It Was* (Fresno, Calif.: Panorama West Publishing, 1976).

Billy J. Peck et al., "Culture Resource Investigations for the North Fork Kern River,
      Tulare and Kern Counties, California," commissioned report by Western
      Ecological Services for the U.S. Forest Service, Sequoia National Forest,
      February 1981, Archaeological and Environmental Services archives, Fresno,
      Calif.

Alfred Pietroforte, *Yokuts and Paiute Songs and Culture* (Happy Camp, Calif.:
      Naturegraph Publishers, 2005).

Stephen Powers, *Tribes of California* (reprint, Berkeley: University of California Press,
      1976).

Linda Reynolds, "Heritage Resources Program Overview, Inyo National Forest,
      California and Nevada," report for U.S. Department of Agriculture, Forest
      Service, Inyo National Forest, 1998, Inyo National Forest archives, Bishop,
      Calif.

Nathan Stevens, "Prehistoric Use of the Alpine Sierra Nevada," master's thesis,
      California State University–Sacramento, 2002.

Francis E. Watkins, "Indians at Play," in *California History Nugget* 7, no. 6 (March
      1940).

7. The Yokuts

1. The valley was near where the town of Coalinga is now.
2. The village was Chuh-muk'-tow, where Springville now lies.
3. Tulare Lake covered a large area of the southern San Joaquin Valley.
4. Frank F. Latta, "The Yauh'-dahn-chees Obtain Fire" in *California Indian Folklore* (Exeter, Calif.: Bear State Books, 1999), 53.
5. A. L. Kroeber, foreword, in Frank F. Latta, *Handbook of Yokuts Indians* (Bakersfield, Calif.: Kern County Museum, 1949).
6. Harold E. Driver, *Culture Element Distributions 6: Southern Sierra Nevada*, University of California Publications in Anthropological Records, vol. 1, bk. 2 (Berkeley: University of California Press, 1937), 86.
7. Latta, *Handbook of Yokuts Indians*, 12.

Additional Sources

Anna H. Gayton, *Yokuts and Western Mono Ethnography: Tulare Lake, Southern Valley, and Central Foothill Yokuts*, University of California Publications in Anthropological Records, vol. 10, bk. 1 (Berkeley: University of California Press, 1948).

A. L. Kroeber, *Elements of Culture in Native California*, University of California Publications in American Archaeology and Ethnology, vol. 13, bk. 8 (Berkeley: University of California Press, 1922).

———, "The Nature of Land-Holding Groups in Aboriginal California," in *Aboriginal California: Three Studies in Culture History* (Berkeley: University of California Press, 1963).

Eugene Menefee and Fred A. Dodge, *History of Tulare and Kings Counties, California*, vol. 12 (Los Angeles: Historic Record Co., 1913).

Robert F. G. Spier, "Foothill Yokuts," in *Handbook of North American Indians*, vol. 8 (Washington, D.C., California Smithsonian Institution, 1978).

Julian H. Steward, *Indian Tribes of Sequoia National Park Region*, bulletin, U.S. Dept. of Interior, National Park Service, Field Division of Education, Berkeley, Calif., 1935.

George W. Stewart, "The Yokuts Indians of the Kaweah Region," in *Sierra Club Bulletin* 12 (1927).

8. The Western Monache

1. Gaylen D. Lee, "The Great Flood," in *Walking Where We Lived: Memoirs of a Mono Indian Family* (Norman: University of Oklahoma Press, 1998), 155–56. Lee recalls a story he heard from a teacher "about a man named Noah who built an ark to protect him, his family, and all of the animals from the great flood. I already knew about the great flood from a story both Grandma and Grandpa told." This selection is his grandparents' story.
2. The name Monache (Monachi) was the original ethnological designation for all prehistoric groups associated with the original Mono Lake Paiute and Owens Valley Paiute, including those who migrated to the west side of the Sierra Nevada. Later, archaeologists and ethnologists separated them into Western Monache and Eastern Monache. Eventually, the Mono Lake Paiute became known as Eastern Monache or Eastern Mono; those on the west side of the Sierra summit were designated Western Monache or Western Mono; the Owens

Valley Paiute designation remained unchanged. Many Western Monache still simply call themselves Monache.

3. George W. Stewart, "The Yokut Indians of the Kaweah Region," *Sierra Club Bulletin* 12 (1927), 392.

4. Edward W. Gifford, *The Northfork Mono*, University of California Publications in American Archaeology and Ethnology, vol. 31, bk. 25 (Berkeley: University of California Press, 1932), 19.

5. As told to Emma Gilliam Crowley by a Western Mono Waksachi Indian who lived on the Kaweah River in the late 1800s. Retold in Alice Gilliam's letter to thirteen-year-old Alice Crowley, April 10, 1908.

6. J. G. Moore and M. F. Diggles, "Hand-hewn Granite Basins at Native American Saltworks, Sierra Nevada, California," U.S. Geographical Survey Scientific Investigations Report 2009-5225, USGS archives, Reston, Va. For over a century, the purposes of large granite bedrock basins that dot the southern Sierra have been debated. Moore and Diggles (2009) determined one extensive group of basins beside a saltwater stream in Miwok territory were used for manufacturing salt.

Additional Sources

Galen Clark, *Indians of the Yosemite Valley and Vicinity* (Yosemite, Calif.: Galen Clark, 1907).

James T. Davis, *Trade Routes and Economic Exchange Among the Indians of California*, Reports of the University of California Archaeological Survey No. 54 (Berkeley: University of California Press, 1961).

Albert B. Elsasser, "Aboriginal Use of Restrictive Sierran Environments," in *Papers on California Archaeology*, University of California Archaeological Survey Report 41 (Berkeley: University of California Press, 1958).

———, *The Archaeology of the Sierra Nevada in California and Nevada*, University of California Archaeological Survey Report 51 (Berkeley: University of California Press, 1960).

Anna H. Gayton, *Yokuts and Western Mono Ethnography: Tulare Lake, Southern Valley, and Central Foothill Yokuts*, University of California Publications in Anthropological Records, vol. 10, bk. 1 (Berkeley: University of California Press, 1948).

———, "Yokuts and Western Mono Social Organizations," in *American Anthropologist* 47, no. 3 (1945).

Infotech Research, "Haas-Kings River Project," report for Pacific Gas & Electric Company, 1985, Pacific Gas & Electric Company archives, San Francisco, Calif.

A. L. Kroeber, *Elements of Culture in Native California*, University of California Publications in American Archaeology and Ethnology, vol. 13, bk. 8 (Berkeley: University of California Press, 1922).

———, "The Nature of Land-Holding Groups in Aboriginal California," in *Aboriginal California: Three Studies in Culture History* (Berkeley: University of California Press, 1963).

Julian H. Steward, *Indian Tribes of Sequoia National Park Region*, bulletin, U.S. Dept. of Interior, National Park Service, Field Division of Education, Berkeley, Calif., 1935.

Douglas Hillman Strong, "A History of Sequoia National Park," abstract of PhD diss., Syracuse University, 1964, Sequoia National Park archives, Three Rivers, Calif.

Wallace B. Woolfenden, "The Role of Social Organization in Trans-Sierran Exchange Systems," unpublished paper, n.d., Inyo National Forest archives, Bishop, Calif.

9. The Sierra Miwok

1. Edward W. Gifford, "The Search for the Deer," in *Miwok Myths*, University of California Publications in American Archaeology and Ethnology, vol. 12, bk. 8 (Berkeley: University of California Press, 1917), 314–18.

2. The Mikow's long digging stick gave them and other foothill people the Euro-American appellation of "Digger Indian." Today the name is often viewed as disparaging.

3. Galen Clark, *Indians of the Yosemite Valley and Vicinity* (Yosemite, Calif.: Galen Clark, 1907), 28.

4. Tina West, "The Life in the Basket," in *Sierra Heritage*, September–October 1997, 27.

5. Clark, *Indians of the Yosemite Valley*, 28.

6. Edward Gifford, *Miwok Cults*, University of California Publications in American Archaeology and Ethnology, vol. 18, bk. 3 (Berkeley: University of California Press, 1926), 395.

7. A. L. Kroeber, *Handbook of the Indians of California* (New York: Dover Publications, 1976), 451.

8. Michael J. Moratto, "Chowchilla River Prehistory," in *The Madera County Historian* 12, no. 2 (April 1972), 3.

Additional Sources

Samuel A. Barrett and Edward W. Gifford, "Miwok Material Culture," in *Bulletin of Milwaukee Public Museum*, March 1933.

Craig D. Bates, "A Historical View of Southern Sierra Miwok Dance and Ceremony," undated manuscript, Yosemite National Park archives, Yosemite, Calif.

Eugene L. Conrotto, *Miwok Means People: The Life and Fate of the Native Inhabitants of the California Gold Rush Country* (Fresno, Calif.: Valley Publishers, 1973).

Edward W. Gifford, *Miwok Moieties*, University of California Publications in American Archaeology and Ethnology, vol. 31, bk. 2 (Berkeley: University of California Press, 1929).

Robert F. Heizer, ed., *Handbook of North American Indians* (Washington, D.C.: Smithsonian Institution, 1978).

Robert F. Heizer and Albert B. Elsasser, *The Natural World of the California Indians* (Berkeley: University of California Press, 1980).

10. The Yosemite

1. Galen Clark, "Legend of To-tau-kon-nu'-la and Tis-sa'-ak," in *Indians of the Yosemite Valley and Vicinity* (Yosemite, Calif.: Galen Clark, 1907), 78–87.

2. Elizabeth Stone O'Neill, *Meadow in the Sky: A History of Yosemite's Tuolumne Meadows Region* (Groveland, Calif.: Albicaulis Press, 1984), 9.

3. Indian names were spelled in different ways by those who heard and used them. The spellings tend to follow either Anglo or Spanish rules of diction as well as personal preference. Thus Ah-wah'ne is also spelled Ah-wah-ne, A-wa'-ni, and Awahni.

4. Elizabeth Godfrey, *Yosemite Indians*, rev. ed. (Yosemite National Park, Calif.: Yosemite Association, 1977), 29–33; Eugene L. Conrotto, *Miwok Means People: The Life and Fate of the Native Inhabitants of the California Gold Rush Country* (Fresno, Calif.: Valley Publishers, 1973), 100. The two versions of the story of El Capitan have variations, as is true of most oral legends recited through the years.
5. Clark, *Indians of the Yosemite Valley*, 63.
6. Conrotto, *Miwok Means People*, 91–92.

Additional Sources

Craig Bates and Martha J. Lee, *Tradition and Innovation* (Yosemite National Park, Calif.: Yosemite Association, 1990).

Elizabeth Godfrey, "Yosemite Indians: Yesterday and Today," in *Yosemite Nature Notes*, special issue, 1951.

Michael J. Moratto, *An Archaeological Design for Yosemite National Park, California*, Western Archaeological and Conservation Center, Publications in Anthropology 19 (Tucson: National Park Service, Western Archaeological and Conservation Center, 1981).

Jean-Nicolas Perlot, *Gold Seeker: Adventures of a Belgian Argonaut During the Gold Rush Years* (New Haven: Yale University Press, 1985).

Stephen Powers, *Tribes of California* (reprint, Berkeley: University of California Press, 1976).

Wallace B. Woolfenden, "The Role of Social Organization in Trans-Sierran Exchange Systems," unpublished paper, n.d., Inyo National Forest archives, Bishop, Calif.

11. The Paiute

1. Many Sierra myths and tales incorporate the concept of reanimation after death.
2. W. A. Chalfant, "Hy-nan-nu," in *The Story of Inyo* (Bishop, Calif.: Chalfant Press, 1933), 58–60: "Cornwell states that there are several Hy-nan-nu legends, forming a character in his progress through the country." The Western Monos also had a Hy-nan-nu legend that corresponded to this one. Others in the Owens Valley had several variations.
3. Charles W. Campbell, "Origins and Ethnography of Prehistoric Man in the Owens Valley," unpublished manuscript, 1974, Eastern California Museum, Bishop, Calif.
4. Also spelled cuzavi, cozaby, kuzabi, or koo-chabie by various ethnologists and writers.
5. Ella M. Cain, *The Story of Early Mono County* (San Francisco: Fearon Publishers, 1961), 103–4; Albert B. Elsasser, "Aboriginal Use of Restrictive Sierran Environments" in Papers on California Archaeology, Reports of the University of California Archaeological Survey No. 41. (Berkeley: University of California Press, 1958), 30.
6. Also spelled piagi or pe'agg-e.
7. I. F. Eldredge, "Caterpillars a la Piute" in *American Forest* 29, no. 354 (1923), 331.
8. The following are Owens Valley Paiute names of several important places: Bishop, *pitana patu* (large village or south place; West Bishop, *paukamatu* (gravel bluff place); Fish Springs, *panatu* (water place) in the agricultural area and *tuniga witu* (around the foot of the mountain place) in the volcanic foothills

above it; Big Pine, *tovowahamatu* (place of big pines); a village near Big Pine, *panapuduhumatu* (unknown meaning); Manzanar, *tupusi* (ground nut place); festival grounds below the dam on "Paiute Ditch," *nugatuhava* (unknown meaning); Baker Creek village, *tovowaha matu* (unknown meaning); Little Pine Creek, *tsagadu* (unknown meaning); Oak Creek, *tsakica witu* (oak place); Independence Creek, *nataka matu* (unknown meaning); Round Valley, *kwina patu* (north place); Birch Mountain, *paukudauwa* or *padkaranwa* (rocky boulder).

9. Philip J. Wilke and Harry W. Lawton, *The Expedition of Capt. J. W. Davidson from Fort Tejon to the Owens Valley in 1859* (Socorro, N. Mex.: Ballena Press, 1976), 7–8.

10. A. L. Kroeber, *Handbook of the Indians of California* (New York: Dover Publications, 1976), 582–83.

11. Wilke and Lawton, *Expedition of Capt. J. W. Davidson*, 30.

12. The following Sierra streams indicate evidence of having been dammed for irrigation: Rock Creek, Pine Creek, Horton Creek, Bishop Creek, Keough Hot Springs [Freeman Creek], Baker Creek, Tinnemaha Creek, Black Rock Spring, Oak Creek, and Independence Creek.

13. Other plants that grew in irrigated fields or in the overflow below them included western yellow cress, love grass, sunflower, water grass (resembling wild oats), white pigweed or goosefoot, clover, blue joint, wheatgrass, Great Basin wild rye, and tobacco.

14. Pitted and scratched forms of petroglyphs may have come from Siberia with the early migrations of prehistoric people to North America, or they may have developed independently in North America.

15. Julian H. Steward, *Petroglyphs of California and Adjoining States*, University of California Publications in American Archaeology and Ethnology, vol. 24, bk. 2 (Berkeley: University of California Press, 1929), 82.

16. Robert F. Heizer and Martin A. Baumhoff, *Prehistoric Rock Art of Nevada and Eastern California* (Berkeley: University of California Press, 1962), 239.

17. Richard Stewart, "The Owens Valley Paiute," unpublished oral history, 1994, Eastern California Museum, Independence, Calif. The tales of the cannibal giant and basket-cap woman are oral stories passed from generation to generation to the present day.

Additional Sources

Edward K. Balls, *Early Uses of California Plants* (Berkeley: University of California Press, 1962).

Warren L. D'Azevedo, ed., *Handbook of North American Indians*, vol. 11, Great Basin (Washington, D.C.: Smithsonian Institution, 1986).

Harold E. Driver, *Culture Element Distributions 6: Southern Sierra Nevada*, University of California Publications in Anthropological Records, vol. 1, bk. 2 (Berkeley: University of California Press, 1937).

Albert B. Elsasser, "Aboriginal Use of Restrictive Sierran Environments," in *Papers on California Archaeology*, University of California Archaeological Survey Report 41 (Berkeley: University of California Press, 1958).

Robert G. Elston, "Prehistory of the Western Area," in *Handbook of North American Indians*, vol. 2, ed. Robert Heizer (Washington, D.C.: Smithsonian Institution, 1878), 135–48.

Robert F. Heizer and C. W. Clewlow, *Prehistoric Rock Art of California*, vol. 1 (Ramona, Calif.: Ballena Press, 1973).

———— and Albert B. Elsasser, *The Natural World of the California Indians* (Berkeley: University of California Press, 1980).

Harry W. Lawton et al., "Agriculture Among the Paiute of Owens Valley," in *Journal of California Anthropology* 3, no. 1 (1976).

William Michaels, "At the Plow and in the Harvest Field: Indian Conflict and Accommodation in the Owens Valley 1860–1880," master's thesis, University of Oklahoma, 1993.

John Miller and Wallace Hutchinson, "Where Pe'ag'gie Manna Falls," in *Nature* 12, no. 3 (September 1928): 158–60.

Linda Reynolds, "Heritage Resources Program Overview, Inyo National Forest, California and Nevada," report for U.S. Department of Agriculture, Forest Service, Inyo National Forest, 1998, Inyo National Forest archives, Bishop, Calif.

Julian H. Steward, *Ethnography of the Owens Valley Paiute*, University of California Publications in American Archaeology and Ethnology, vol. 33, bk. 3 (Berkeley: University of California Press, 1933).

————, "Panatubiji, an Owens Valley Paiute," *Bureau of American Ethnology Bulletin* 119, no. 6 (1938).

Omar C. Stewart, *Two Paiute Autobiographies*, University of California Publications in American Archaeology and Ethnology, vol. 33, bk. 5 (Berkeley: University of California Press, 1934).

Wallace B. Woolfenden, "The Role of Social Organization in Trans-Sierran Exchange Systems," unpublished paper, n.d., Inyo National Forest archives, Bishop, Calif.

Elva Younkin, ed., *Coso Rock Art: A New Perspective* (Ridgecrest, Calif.: Maturango Press, 1998).

Epilogue

1.   Frank F. Latta, "The Bird and Animal People Leave," in *California Indian Folklore* (Exeter, Calif.: Bear State Books, 1999).

Additional Sources

John Francis Bannon, ed., *Bolton and the Spanish Borderlands* (Norman: University of Oklahoma Press, 1964).

Joe Doctor, "Spanish Exploratory Expeditions to Kaweah," in *Sun, Herald, Echo*, n.d., 1987.

Michael Mathes, *Spanish Approaches to the Island of California 1628–1632* (San Francisco: Book Club of California, 1975).

Ardis Manly Walker, *Francisco Garces: A Pioneer Padre of Los Tulares* (Bakersfield, Calif.: Kern County Historical Society and the County of Kern, 1946).

Acknowledgements

In a book that examines the lives and events of ancient beings, the search for truth is elusive. The stories of their existence can only be imagined from scant physical artifacts and oral traditions that have been modified through the centuries. To those who have generously provided their professional viewpoints and expertise go my heartfelt thanks.

Among those I wish to thank especially are: Clifford Hopson, geology professor emeritus at University of California, Santa Barbara, who gave countless hours of his time, encouragement, knowledge, reference materials, and critical acumen to the project; Tom Burge, Sequoia National Park Archeologist, for opening his personal photograph files and for his detailed review of the prehistoric peoples portion of the manuscript; Joel Despain, Sequoia National Park geologist and cave specialist, for his review of the geology chapters and references; V. Scott Moore, engineering geologist, for his review and edits; Dan Voelz, geography professor, Fresno State University, who provided his geology expertise on a walk in the southern Sierra wilderness.

Special thanks to: Wallace Woolfenden, paleoecologist, Heritage Resource Management, for his time, interest, sharing of information, photographs, and valuable resources, and his critical review of the entire manuscript; Richard Burns, retired naturalist, Sequoia National Park, who also reviewed the entire manuscript; Linda Reynolds, Inyo National Forest archaeologist, for her materials, references, and editing; Nathan Stevens, archaeologist, for his fresh perspective and help; Chris Brewer, historian and publisher, who opened his private collection to me for my research; historian Bill Horst, who shared his collection of oral histories and data from field explorations; Manuel

Andrade and Gordon Retfeldt, who provided an amazing field day exploring pictographs in the foothills of the southern Sierra; Laurel, Laile, and Brian DiSilvestro, for their incredible encouragement and hours of help with all facets of the project.

Others who perused their files to provide the research materials, photographs, maps, and diagrams so essential to the book include: Willem Kerwin, Inyo National Forest archives; Ward Eldredge, Sequoia National Park archivist; Kirk Halford and Mike Holt, Bureau of Land Management, Bishop Field Office archives; Beth Porter, Eastern California Museum, and Kathy McGowan, Tulare County Museum, who both opened their cases of prehistoric artifacts for photographs; Sierra photographers Fred Reimer and Dan Hammond.

Much appreciation to the libraries and museums that provided research material for the book, especially to some of the contacts who were most helpful: Keith Pringle, Ardis Walker Library, Kernville, California; staff, Bancroft Library, University of California, Berkeley; staff, California State Library, Sacramento; Bill Michaels and Kathy Barnes, Eastern California Museum, Independence; Sara Sutton, Tulare County Office of Education, Visalia, California; staff, Inyo County Library, Bishop and Independence, California; Linda Reynolds and Jan Cutts, Inyo National Forest Archives, Bishop, California; staff, Laws Railroad Museum, Laws (Bishop), California; Elva Younkin, Maturango Museum Library, Ridgecrest, California; Stephanie Hungate, Sequoia National Forest Archives, Porterville, California; Tom Nave, Sierra National Forest Archives, Clovis, California; staff, Three Rivers Historical Society Museum and Archives, Three Rivers, California; Mary Ann Terstegge and Terry Ommen, Tulare County Library, Visalia, California; staff, Special Collections, University of Nevada, Reno; Jim Snyder and Linda Eade, Yosemite National Park Archives and Library, Yosemite, California.

Bibliography

Published Materials

Alt, David D., and Donald W. Hyndman. *Roadside Geology of Northern California*. Missoula, Mont.: Mountain Press Publishing, 1975.

———. *Roadside Geology of Northern and Central California*. Missoula, Mont.: Mountain Press Publishing, 2000.

Associated Press. "Sierra Older, Higher Than Once Believed." Reprinted in *Inyo Register*, June 17, 1996.

Bailey, Edgar H., ed. *Geology of Northern California*. California Division of Mines and Geology Bulletin 190. San Francisco: California Division of Mines and Geology, 1966.

Bakker, Elna S. *An Island Called California: An Ecological Introduction to Its Natural Communities*. Berkeley: University of California Press, 1971.

Ballew, Dixie Clarkson. "The Indians of Lemon Cove." In *Tulare County Historical Society Newsletter*, October 1969.

Balls, Edward K. *Early Uses of California Plants*. Berkeley: University of California Press, 1962.

Bannon, John Francis, ed. *Bolton and the Spanish Borderlands*. Norman: University of Oklahoma Press, 1964.

Barrett, Samuel A., and Edward W. Gifford. "Miwok Material Culture." In *Bulletin of Milwaukee Public Museum*, March 1933. Reprinted as *Indian Life of the Yosemite Region*. Pamphlet. Yosemite National Park, Calif.: Yosemite Association, n.d.

Bateman, Paul C. "Geologic Structure and History of the Sierra Nevada." In *UMR (University of Missouri–Rolla) Journal* 1 (April 1968): 121–31.

Bates, Craig D. "Fish and the Miwok." In *Masterkey* 58, no. 1 (Spring 1984): 18–23.

———, and Martha J. Lee. *Tradition and Innovation*. Yosemite National Park, Calif.: Yosemite Association, 1990.

Baumhoff, Martin A. *Ecological Determinants of Aboriginal California Populations*. University of California Publications in American Archaeology and Ethnology, vol. 49, bk. 2. Berkeley: University of California Press, 1963.

Beck, Warren A., and Ynez D. Haase. *Historical Atlas of California*. Norman: University of Oklahoma Press, 1974.

Bent, Arthur Cleveland. *Life Histories of North American Birds of Prey*. 2 vols. New York: Dover Publications, 1961.

Bott, Martin H. P. *The Interior of the Earth: Its Structure, Constitution and Evolution*. New York: Elsevier Science Publishing, 1982.

Bradigan, Bret. "Kern River Valley Indian Community: A Historical Overview, Prehistory to 1863." Series of articles in *Kern Valley Sun*, Kernville, Calif., n.d.

Brewer, William H. *Up and Down California in 1860–1864*. New Haven: Yale University Press, 1930. Reprint, Berkeley: University of California Press, 1966.

Britten, Sophronia. "Last of the California Grizzlies." In *Three Rivers Historical Society Newsletter*, Spring 2002.

Brown, Vincent, and Robert Livezey. *The Sierra Nevadan Wildlife Region*. Healdsburg, Calif.: Naturegraph Co., 1962.

Bunnel, Lafayette Houghton. *Discovery of the Yosemite and the Indian War of 1851*. Los Angeles: G. W. Gerlicher, 1911. Reprint, Yosemite, Calif.: Yosemite Association, 1990.

Burge, Thomas L. "Native American Sites Discovered." In *Seedlings*, November 2001.

Burmeister, Eugene. *Early Days in Kern*. Bakersfield, Calif.: Cardon House, 1963.

Burnham, Don. "Owens Valley's Indian Heritage." In *Sierra Life* 3, no. 2 (November/ December 1988).

Busby-Spera, Cathy, and Jason Saleeby. *Geologic Guide to the Mineral King Area, Sequoia National Park, California*. Los Angeles, Calif.: Pacific Section of Economic Paleontologists and Mineralogists, 1987.

Bush, Elsie. "Archaeological Sites are Catalogued." In *Fresno Bee*, November 8, 1974.

Cabrera, Luis. "Bones Identified as Native to Area." In *Reno Gazette-Journal*, January 14, 2000.

Cain, Ella M. *The Story of Early Mono County*. San Francisco: Fearon Publishers, 1961.

Castellon, David. "Where's our Moho?" In *Visalia Times-Delta*, Weekend Edition, October 2 and 3, 2004.

Chalfant, W. A. *The Story of Inyo*. Bishop, Calif.: Chalfant Press, 1933.

Chase, Clyde Scott. "The Forest Kings: An Account of the Mighty Sequoias of California." In *Harper's Illustrated Weekly Magazine*, December 17, 1905.

Clark, Galen. *Indians of the Yosemite Valley and Vicinity*. Yosemite, Calif.: Galen Clark, 1907.

Clark, Lewis. *Animals of the Sequoia-Kings Canyon Country*. San Bruno, Calif.: Lewis Clark, 1957.

Clarke, Graham. "Ecological Zones and Economic Stages." In *Prehistoric Europe: The Economic Basis*. London and Stanford, Calif.: Methuen & Company and Stanford University Press, 1952. Reprinted in *Man in Adaptation: The Biosocial Background*. Edited by Yehudi A. Cohen. Chicago: Aldine Publishing, 1968.

Cole, James E. *Cone-bearing Trees of Yosemite National Park*. Yosemite National Park, Calif.: Yosemite Natural History Association, 1963.

Conrotto, Eugene L. *Miwok Means People: The Life and Fate of the Native Inhabitants of the California Gold Rush Country*. Fresno, Calif.: Valley Publishers, 1973.

Cook, S. F. "The Mechanism and Extent of Dietary Adaptation Among Certain Groups of California and Nevada Indians." In *Ibero-Americana*. Berkeley: University of California Press, 1941.

Cox, John D. "Ancient Trees Help Unravel Tahoe Climate Mystery." From *Sacramento Bee*. Reprinted in *Reno Gazette-Journal*, January 9, 2000.

Cronise, Titus Fey. *The Natural Wealth of California.* San Francisco: H. H. Bancroft & Co., 1868.

Davis, James T. *Trade Routes and Economic Exchange Among the Indians of California.* Reports of the University of California Archaeological Survey No. 54. Berkeley: University of California Press, 1961.

D'Azevedo, Warren L., ed. *Handbook of North American Indians.* Vol. 11, *Great Basin.* Washington, D.C.: Smithsonian Institution, 1986.

Despain, Joel. *Hidden Beneath the Mountains.* Dayton, Ohio: Cave Books, 2003.

Dilsaver, Larry M., and William C. Tweed. *Challenge of the Big Trees: A Resource History of Sequoia and Kings Canyon National Parks.* Three Rivers, Calif.: Sequoia Natural History Association, 1990.

Doctor, Joe. "Archaeologists Had Interesting Time Exploring Damsite." In *Sun, Herald, Echo,* January 21, 1987.

———. "California Yokuts Indian Language Traced to Siberia." In *Sun, Herald, Echo,* December 26, 1984.

———. "Exeter Rocky Hill." In *Los Tulares* 172 (June 1991).

———. "Rock Basins Studied for Traces of Early-Day Civilization in County." In *Exeter Sun,* October 1958.

———. "Spanish Exploratory Expeditions to Kaweah." In *Sun, Herald, Echo,* n.d., 1987.

———. "Wahnomcot Pronounced Name of River Correctly." In *Sun, Herald, Echo,* January 14, 1987.

———. "Wukchumni, Padwisha Indians Lived Along River." In *Sun, Herald, Echo,* January 7, 1987.

Dowdell, Dorothy and Joseph. *Sierra Nevada: The Golden Barrier.* New York: Bobbs Merrill, 1968.

Driver, Harold E. *Culture Element Distributions 6: Southern Sierra Nevada.* University of California Publications in Anthropological Records, vol. 1, bk. 2. Berkeley: University of California Press, 1937.

Dulitz, David. Presentation for Tulare County Historical Society field trip, Mountain Home State Forest, California, August 11, 2007. Audiotape.

Eldredge, I. F. "Caterpillars a la Piute." In *American Forest* 29, no. 354 (1923): 330–32.

Elliott, Wallace W., and Company. *History of Tulare County California with Illustrations.* San Francisco: Wallace W. Elliott & Co., 1883.

Elsasser, Albert B. "Aboriginal Use of Restrictive Sierran Environments." In *Papers on California Archaeology.* Reports of the University of California Archaeological Survey No. 41. Berkeley: University of California Press, 1958.

———. *The Archaeology of the Sierra Nevada in California and Nevada.* Reports of the University of California Archaeological Survey No. 51. Berkeley: University of California Press, 1960.

———. *Indians of Sequoia and Kings Canyon National Parks.* Three Rivers, Calif.: Sequoia Natural History Association, 1962.

Farquhar, Francis P. "Exploration of the Sierra Nevada." In *California Historical Society Quarterly* 5 (March 1925).

———. *History of the Sierra Nevada.* Berkeley: University of California Press, 1965.

Fatooh, Joy. "My Mountain Is Always Good to Me." In *The Album* 2 (April 11, 1989).

Fenega, Franklin. "The Archaeology of the Slick Rock Village, Tulare County, California." In *American Antiquity* 4, 1952.

Gayton, Anna H. *Yokuts and Western Mono Ethnography: Tulare Lake, Southern Valley, and Central Foothill Yokuts.* University of California Publications in Anthropological Records, vol. 10, bk. 1. Berkeley: University of California Press, 1948.

————. *Yokuts and Western Mono Pottery-Making.* University of California Publications in American Archaeology and Ethnology, vol. 24, bk. 3. Berkeley: University of California Press, 1929.

————. "Yokuts and Western Mono Social Organization." In *American Anthropologist* 47, no. 3 (1945): 409–26.

————. *Yokuts-Mono Chiefs and Shamans.* University of California Publications in American Archaeology and Ethnology, vol. 24, bk. 8. Berkeley: University of California Press, 1930.

Gibbons, Ann. "Food for Thought." In *Science* 316 (June 1, 2007): 1558–60.

Gifford, Edward Winslow. *California Kinship Terminologies.* University of California Publications in American Archaeology and Ethnology, vol. 18, bk. 1. Berkeley: University of California Press, 1922.

————. *Miwok Cults.* University of California Publications in American Archaeology and Ethnology, vol. 18, bk. 3. Berkeley: University of California Press, 1926.

————. *Miwok Moieties.* University of California Publications in American Archaeology and Ethnology, vol. 31, bk. 2. Berkeley: University of California Press, 1929.

————. *Miwok Myths.* University of California Publications in American Archaeology and Ethnology, vol. 12, bk. 8. Berkeley: University of California Press, 1917.

————. *The Northfork Mono.* University of California Publications in American Archaeology and Ethnology, vol. 31, bk. 25. Berkeley: University of California Press, 1932.

————. *Tubatulabal and Kawaiisu Kinship Terms.* University of California Publications in American Archaeology and Ethnology, vol. 12, bk. 6. Berkeley: University of California Press, 1917.

Gilbert, G. K. "The Moulin, or Glacial Mill." Report for U.S. Geological Survey, 1906. Published in *Glaciological Notes* 54 (Fall/Winter 1973).

Gilligan, D. *The Secret Sierra: The Alpine World Above the Trees.* Bishop, Calif.: Spotted Dog Press, 2000.

Godfrey, Elizabeth. *Yosemite Indians.* Revised edition. Yosemite National Park, Calif.: Yosemite Association, 1977.

————. "Yosemite Indians: Yesterday and Today." In *Yosemite Nature Notes.* Special issue, 1951.

Grinnell, Joseph, Joseph Dixon, and Jean Linsdale. *Fur Bearing Mammals of California.* Vol. 1. Berkeley: University of California Press, 1937.

Heizer, Robert F., ed. *Handbook of North American Indians.* Vol. 8, *California.* Washington, D.C.: Smithsonian Institution, 1978.

————. *Languages, Territories, and Names of California Indian Tribes.* Berkeley: University of California Press, 1966.

————, and Martin A. Baumhoff. *Prehistoric Rock Art of Nevada and Eastern California.* Berkeley: University of California Press, 1962.

————, and C. W. Clewlow. *Prehistoric Rock Art of California.* Vol 1. Ramona, Calif.: Ballena Press, 1973.

Heizer, Robert F., and Albert B. Elsasser. *The Natural World of the California Indians*. Berkeley: University of California Press, 1980.

Hill, Mary. *California Landscape: Origin and Evolution*. California Natural History Guide 48. Berkeley: University of California Press, 1984.

———. *Geology of the Sierra Nevada*. Berkeley: University of California Press, 1975.

Hinds, Norman. *Evolution of the California Landscape*. California Division of Mines and Geology Bulletin 158. San Francisco: California Division of Mines and Geology, 1952.

Horn, Elizabeth L. *Sierra Nevada Wildflowers*. Missoula, Mont.: Mountain Press Publishing, 1998.

Hough, Susan Elizabeth. *Finding Fault in California*. Missoula, Mont.: Mountain Press Publishing, 2004.

Howard, Thomas F. *Sierra Crossing*. Berkeley: University of California Press, 1998.

Hull, Kathleen L. "The Sierra Nevada: Archaeology in the Range of Light." In *California Prehistory: Colonization, Culture and Complexity*. Edited by Terry Jones and Kathryn Klan. Walnut Creek, Calif.: Alta Mira Press, 2007.

———, et al. "Prehistoric Economic Systems." In *Archeological Synthesis and Research Design*. Yosemite Research Center Publications in Anthropology 21. Yosemite, Calif.: National Park Service, Yosemite Research Center, 1999.

Hundley, Norris, Jr. *The Great Thirst: Californians and Water, 1770s–1990s*. Berkeley: University of California Press, 1992.

Ingles, Lloyd Glenn. *Mammals of California*. Stanford: Stanford University Press, 1947.

Jameson, W. W., Jr., and Hans J. Peeters. *California Mammals*. Berkeley: University of California Press, 1988.

Jenkins, J. C., and Ruby Johnson Jenkins. *Exploring the Southern Sierra: Eastside*. Berkeley, Calif.: Wilderness Press, 1988.

———. *Exploring the Southern Sierra: Westside*. Berkeley, Calif.: Wilderness Press, 1995.

Jenkins, J. C., and John W. Robinson. *Kern Peak–Olancha*. High Sierra Hiking Guide 13. Berkeley, Calif.: Wilderness Press, 1973.

Johnston, Verna R. *Sierra Nevada: The Naturalist's Companion*. Revised Edition. Berkeley: University of California Press, 1998. Originally published as *Sierra Nevada: The Naturalist's America*. Boston: Houghton Mifflin, 1970.

Jones, Craig, Jeffrey R. Unruh, and Leslie J. Sancher. "The Role of Gravitational Potential Energy in the Active Deformation in the Southwestern United States." In *Nature* 381, no. 6577 (May 2, 1996): 37–41.

Kelly, Isabel T. *Southern Paiute Shamanism*. University of California Publications in Anthropological Records, vol. 2, bk. 4. Berkeley: University of California Press, 1939.

Kerr, Mark. "The Shoshoni Indians of Inyo County, California." In *The Kerr Manuscript*. Edited by Charles N. Irwin. Menlo Park, Calif.: Ballena Press, 1980.

Kerr, Richard A. "New Data Hint at Why Earth Hums and Mountains Rise." In *Science* 283 (January 15, 1999): 320–24.

Kientz, Marvin L. *Indians of the Sierra Foothills*. Porterville, Calif.: Three Forests Interpretive Association, 2002.

King, Clarence. *Mountaineering in the Sierra Nevada*. Boston: James R. Osgood & Co., 1872. Reprint, Lincoln: University of Nebraska Press, 1970.

Konigsmark, Ted. *Geologic Trips: Sierra Nevada*. Gualala, Calif.: GeoPress, 2002.
Kottak, Conrad Phillip. *Anthropology: The Exploration of Human Diversity*. 2nd edition. New York: Random House, 1978.
Kroeber, A. L. *Elements of Culture in Native California*. University of California Publications in American Archaeology and Ethnology, vol. 13, bk. 8. Berkeley: University of California Press, 1922.
———. *Handbook of the Indians of California*. New York: Dover Publications, 1976. Originally published 1925 by U.S. Government Printing Office as *Bureau of American Ethnology of the Smithsonian Institution Bulletin 78*.
———. "The Nature of Land-Holding Groups in Aboriginal California." Report of the University of California Archaeological Survey No. 56. In *Aboriginal California: Three Studies in Culture History*. Berkeley: University of California Press, 1963.
Lange, Arthur L. "Caves of the Southern Sierra in the Geologic Record." In *Caves of the Sequoia Region, California*. National Speleological Society Guide Book No. 7. Edited by Richard J. Reardon. Washington D.C.: National Speleological Society, 1966.
Lanning, Edward P. *Archaeology of the Rose Spring Site: INY 372*. University of California Publications in American Archaeology and Ethnology, vol. 49, bk. 3. Berkeley: University of California Press, 1963.
Latta, Frank F. *California Indian Folklore*. Shafter, Calif.: Frank F. Latta, 1936. Reprint, Exeter, Calif.: Bear State Books, 1999.
———. *Handbook of Yokuts Indians*. Bakersfield, Calif.: Kern County Museum, 1949.
———. *Saga of Rancho El Tejon*. Bakersfield, Calif.: Bear State Books, 1976.
Lawson, Andrew Cowper. *The Geomorphogeny of the Upper Kern Basin*. University of California Publications in Geological Sciences, vol. 3, bk. 15. Berkeley: University of California Press, 1904.
Lawton, Harry W., et al. "Agriculture among the Paiute of Owens Valley." In *Journal of California Anthropology* 3, no. 1 (1976): 13–50.
Leakey, Neave. "The Dawn of Humans." In *National Geographic* 188 (September 1995): 38–51.
Le Conte, Joseph N. "The High Sierra of California." In *Alpina Americana* 1 (1907): 1–16.
———. "Theory of the Formation of the Great Features of Earth's Surface." In *A Century of Science in America*. New Haven: Yale University Press, 1918.
Lee, Gaylen D. *Walking Where We Lived: Memoirs of a Mono Indian Family*. Norman: University of Oklahoma Press, 1998.
Lee, Jim. "Early Sierra Indians." In *Fresno State University Mountain Press*, newsletter no. 10 (April 1985).
———, et al. "Osmium Isotopic Evidence for Mesozoic Removal of Lithospheric Mantle Beneath the Sierra Nevada, California." In *Science*, September 15, 2000.
Livermore, Norman B., Jr. "Collecting Sierra Passes." In *Sierra Club Bulletin* 27, no. 4 (August 1942).
Los Angeles Times. "Bones Found Off California Coast Might Help Rewrite North American History." Reprinted in *Reno Gazette-Journal*, April 11, 1999.
Los Angeles Times. "DNA Links Descendants of Chumash." Reprinted in *Visalia Times-Delta*, September 12, 2006.
"Mammoth Tusks at Mooney Museum." In *Los Tulares* 157 (September 1987): 2.

Mann, Charles C. "America's Pristine Myth." In *Christian Science Monitor,* September 1, 2005.

Mathes, Michael. *Spanish Approaches to the Island of California 1628–1632.* San Francisco: Book Club of California, 1975.

Matsch, Charles L. *North America and the Great Ice Age.* New York: McGraw-Hill, 1976.

Matthes, Francois E. "Geologic History of Mt. Whitney." In *Francois Matthes and the Marks of Time: Yosemite and the High Sierra.* Edited by Fritiof Fryxell. San Francisco: Sierra Club, 1962.

———. *The Incomparable Valley: A Geologic Interpretation of the Yosemite.* Berkeley: University of California Press, 1950.

———. *Sequoia National Park: A Geological Album.* Berkeley: University of California Press, 1950.

McCarthy, Helen C., Clinton M. Blount, and R. A. Hicks. "A Functional Analysis of Bedrock Mortars: Western Mono Food Processing in the Southern Sierra Nevada." Appendix F in *Ethnographic, Historic, and Archaeological Overviews and Archaeological Survey.* Vol. 1 of *Cultural Resources of the Crane Valley Hydroelectric Project Area, Madera County, California.* Commissioned report by Infotec Research, Sonora, Calif., for Pacific Gas & Electric Company, San Francisco, 1985. Sierra National Forest archives, Clovis, Calif.

McClatchy-Tribune. "Ancient Hot Spell May Hold Clues to Warming." In *Visalia Times Delta,* weekend edition, August 26 and 27, 2006.

McLean, Dewey M. "The Deccan Traps Volcanism-Greenhouse Dinosaur Extinction Theory." In *Journal of Geological Education* 43 (1996): 517–28.

Menefee, Eugene, and Fred A. Dodge. *History of Tulare and Kings Counties, California.* Vol. 12. Los Angeles: Historic Record Co., 1913.

Merriam, C. Hart. "Distribution of Indian Tribes in the Southern Sierra and Adjacent Parts of the San Joaquin Valley, California." In *Science* 19, no. 494 (June 17, 1904): 912–17.

———. *Ethnographic Notes on California Indian Tribes.* Edited by Robert E. Heizer. Reports of the University of California Archaeological Survey No. 68. Berkeley: University of California Press, 1967.

Miller, John, and Wallace Hutchinson. "Where Pe'ag'gie Manna Falls." In *Nature* 12, no. 3 (September 1928): 158–60.

Miller, Thelma B. *History of Kern County California.* Vol. 1. Chicago: S. J. Clarke Publishing, 1929.

Mitchell, Annie. "Indian Rock Basins Found Only in County." In *Visalia Times-Delta,* n.d.

———. *The Way It Was.* Fresno, Calif.: Panorama West Publishing, 1976.

Moody, Warren G. *Outdoor Insight from Deer Creek Canyon and California Hot Springs to the Kern River Plateau and Mt. Whitney, and Ways of Mountain Men.* Porterville, Calif.: Andiron Publications, 1986. Originally self-published 1919.

Moore, James G. *Exploring the Highest Sierra.* Stanford: Stanford University Press, 2000.

———, and M. F. Diggles. "Hand-hewn Granite Basins at Native American Saltworks, Sierra Nevada, California." U.S. Geographical Survey Scientific Investigations Report 2009-5225. USGS archives, Reston, Va.

Moorehead, Mary Thul. *Archaeological Survey of the Mineral King Road Corridor.* Tucson: Western Archaeological Center, National Park Service, 1975.

Moratto, Michael J. *An Archaeological Design for Yosemite National Park, California.* Western Archaeological and Conservation Center, Publications in Anthropology 19. Tucson: National Park Service, Western Archaeological and Conservation Center, 1981.

———. *California Archaeology.* Orlando: Academic Press, 1984.

———. "Chowchilla River Prehistory." In *The Madera County Historian* 12, no. 2 (April 1972).

Muir, John. "Gentle Wilderness: The Sierra Nevada." Edited by David Brower. New York: Promontory Press, 1967.

———. *The Mountains of California.* New York: The Century Co., 1894.

———. *Picturesque California and the Region West of the Rocky Mountains, from Alaska to Mexico.* 2 vols. San Francisco: J. Dewing and Company, 1888–90. Reprinted as *West of the Rocky Mountains.* Philadelphia: Running Press, 1976.

———. *South of Yosemite: Selected Writings.* Edited by Frederick R. Gunsky. For the American Museum of Natural History. Garden City, N.Y.: Natural History Press, 1968.

Nelson, C. A., et al. *Guidebook to the Geology of a Portion of the Eastern Sierra Nevada, Owens Valley and White-Inyo Range.* Esso Guidebook 12, Department of Earth and Space Sciences, University of California–Los Angeles, 1980.

New York Times. "Study: Mass Extinction Didn't Give Rise to Mammals." Reprinted in *Visalia Times Delta*, March 29, 2007.

Oakeshott, Gordon B. *California's Changing Landscapes.* New York: McGraw-Hill, 1978.

O'Neill, Elizabeth Stone. *Meadow in the Sky: A History of Yosemite's Tuolumne Meadows Region.* Groveland, Calif.: Albicaulis Press, 1984.

Otter, Floyd L. *The Men of Mammoth Forest.* Porterville, Calif.: Floyd L. Otter, 1963.

Pakiser, L. C. "Seismic Models of the Root of the Sierra Nevada." In *Science* 210 (December 5, 1980).

Paleontology Research Group, Dept. of Geology. *Paleofiles.* Bristol, UK: University of Bristol, 2006. Accessed online at www.bristol.ac.uk.

Parcher, Frank M. "They Will Eat the Food of Their Fathers." In *Los Angeles Times Sunday Magazine*, July 5, 1931.

Paruk, Jim. *Sierra Nevada Tree Identifier.* Yosemite, Calif.: Yosemite Natural History Association, 1997.

Peattie, Roderick, ed. *The Sierra Nevada: Range of Light.* New York: Vanguard Press, 1947.

Perlman, David. "Molten Rock May Hold Key to Rise of High Sierra." In *San Francisco Chronicle*, July 30, 2004.

Perlot, Jean-Nicolas. *Gold Seeker: Adventures of a Belgian Argonaut During the Gold Rush Years.* New Haven: Yale University Press, 1985.

Peterson, P. Victor, and P. Victor Peterson, Jr. *Native Trees of the Sierra Nevada.* Berkeley: University of California Press, 1975.

Petit, Charles. "Earth's Wobble May Be Cause of Ice Ages." In *San Francisco Chronicle*, January 16, 1996.

Phillips, Bill. "Did Prehistoric Moonshiners Roam Through Tulare County?" In *Visalia Times Delta*, July 1, 1974.

"Pictograph." In *Los Tulares* 140 (September 1983): 1–2.

Pietroforte, Alfred. *Yokuts and Paiute Songs and Culture*. Happy Camp, Calif.: Naturegraph Publishers, 2005.

Pilling, Arnold R. "The Archeological Implications of an Annual Coastal Visit for Certain Yokuts Groups." In *American Anthropologist* 52 (1950): 438–40.

Powers, Bob. *Indian Country of the Tubatulabal*. Los Angeles: Westernlore Press, 1981.

Powers, Stephen. *Tribes of California*. Vol. 3 of *Contributions to North American Ethnology*. Washington, D.C.: U.S. Government Printing Office, 1877. Reprint, Berkeley: University of California Press, 1976.

Press, Frank, and Raymond Siever. *Understanding Earth*. New York: W. H. Freeman & Co., 1994.

Ratliff, Raymond D. *Meadows in the Sierra Nevada of California: State of Knowledge*. General Technical Report PSW-84, U.S. Department of Agriculture, Forest Service. Berkeley, Calif.: Pacific Southwest Forest and Range Experiment Station, 1985.

Ritchie, David. *Superquake! Why Earthquakes Occur and When the Big One Will Hit Southern California*. New York: Crown Publishers, 1988.

Rowe, Jason. "The Last Day in the Life of a Miwok Boy." In *The Sentinel* 2 (Spring 1974).

Runte, Alfred. *Yosemite: The Embattled Wilderness*. Lincoln: University of Nebraska Press, 1990.

Russell, Israel C. *Quaternary History of the Mono Valley*. Lee Vining, Calif.: Artemisia Press, 1984. Originally published 1889 by U.S. Government Printing Office in *Eighth Annual Report of the U.S. Geological Survey*.

Saleeby, Jason B. *Field Trip Guide to the Kings-Kaweah Suture, Southwestern Sierra Foothills, California*. Guidebook prepared for the 73rd Annual Meeting of the Cordilleran Section, Geological Society of America, April 1977.

———. "On Some Aspects of the Geology of the Sierra Nevada." In *Classic Cordilleran Concepts: A View From California*. Special Paper 338. Boulder, Colo.: Geological Society of America, 1999.

Sample, L. L. *Trade and Trails in Aboriginal California*. Reports of the University of California Archaeological Survey No. 8. Berkeley: University of California Press, 1950.

Sanborn, Margaret. *Yosemite: Its Discovery, Its Wonders, and Its People*. Yosemite National Park, Calif.: Yosemite Association, 1989.

Schaffer, Jeffrey P. *The Geomorphic Evolution of the Yosemite Valley and Sierra Nevada Landscapes*. Berkeley, Calif.: Wilderness Press, 1997.

Schoenherr, Allan A. *A Natural History of California*. California Natural History Guides. Berkeley: University of California Press, 1992.

Seton-Thompson, Ernest. *The Biography of a Grizzly*. New York: The Century Company, 1899.

Seyfert, Carl K., and Leslie A. Sirkin. *Earth History and Plate Tectonics: An Introduction to Historical Geology*. New York: Harper & Row, 1973.

Sheehan, Jack R. "Tectonic Overview of Owens Valley Region." In *Guidebook to the Eastern Sierra Nevada, Owens Valley, White-Inyo Range*. Edited by C. A. Nelson. Los Angeles: University of California–Los Angeles, Department of Earth and Space Sciences, 1980.

Shirley, James Clifford. *The Redwoods of Coast and Sierra*. Berkeley: University of California Press, 1940.

"Sierra Nevada Range on the Move." In *Kaweah Commonwealth*, May 10, 1996.

Simmons, William S. "Indian Peoples of California." In *Contested Eden: California Before the Gold Rush*. Edited by Ramon Gutierrez and Richard Orsi. California History Sesquicentennial Series 1. Berkeley: University of California Press in association with California Historical Society, 1997.

Sion, Mike. "Seismic Find Rocks Theories." In *Reno Gazette Journal*, November 7, 1994.

Skinner, John H. "Placer Big Trees." In *Sierra Heritage*, May–June 2005.

Small, Kathleen Edwards. *History of Tulare County, California*. Vol. 1. Chicago: S. J. Clarke, 1926.

Spotts, Peter N. "First Americans May Have Crossed Atlantic 50,000 Years Ago." In *Christian Science Monitor*, November 18, 2004.

———. "Fossil Fills Gap in Move from Sea to Land." In *Christian Science Monitor*, April 5, 2006.

Steward, Julian H. *Ethnography of the Owens Valley Paiute*. University of California Publications in American Archaeology and Ethnology, vol. 33, bk. 3. Berkeley: University of California Press, 1933.

———. *Indian Tribes of Sequoia National Park Region*. Bulletin, U.S. Dept. of Interior, National Park Service, Field Division of Education, Berkeley, Calif., 1935.

———. "Panatubiji, an Owens Valley Paiute." In *Bureau of American Ethnology Bulletin* 119, no. 6 (1938).

———. *Petroglyphs of California and Adjoining States*. University of California Publications in American Archaeology and Ethnology, vol. 24, bk. 2. Berkeley: University of California Press, 1929.

Stewart, George W. "Prehistoric Rock Basins in the Sierra Nevada." In *American Anthropology* 31, no. 3 (1929): 419–40.

———. "The Yokuts Indians of the Kaweah Region." In *Sierra Club Bulletin* 12 (1927): 385–400.

Stewart, Omar C. *Two Paiute Autobiographies*. University of California Publications in American Archaeology and Ethnology, vol. 33, bk. 5. Berkeley: University of California Press, 1934. Reprint. Berkeley: University of California Press, 1978.

Storer, Tracy I., and Lloyd P. Tevis, Jr. *California Grizzly*. Berkeley: University of California Press, 1955.

Storer, Tracy I., and Robert L. Usinger. *Sierra Nevada Natural History*. Berkeley: University of California Press, 1963.

Strong, W. D. "Indian Records of California Carnivores." In *Journal of Mammalogy* 7, no. 59 (1926).

Sumner, Lowell, and Joseph S. Dixon. *Birds and Mammals of the Sierra Nevada*. Berkeley: University of California Press, 1953.

Tarling, Don, and Maureen Tarling. *Continental Drift: A Study of the Earth's Moving Surface*. Garden City, N.Y.: Doubleday & Co., 1971.

Taylor, Ron. "Sierra Skeletons May Reveal Story of Monos, Early Whites." *Fresno Bee*, March 31, 1960.

Thomas, John Hunter, and Dennis R. Parnell. *Native Shrubs of the Sierra Nevada*. California Natural History Guides. Berkeley: University of California Press, 1974.

Trexler, Keith A. *The Tioga Road: A History*. Yosemite National Park, Calif.: Yosemite Natural History Association, n.d.

University of California, SNEP Science Team, and Special Consultants. *Sierra Nevada Ecosystem Project*. 3 vols. Commissioned report for U.S. Congress. Davis, Calif.: Centers for Water and Wildland Resources, University of California–Davis, 1996.

U.S. Department of Agriculture. Weather Bureau. *Climatic Summary of the United States, Section 17-Central California.* Edited by J. R. Martin. Washington, D.C.: U.S. Government Printing Office, 1930.

U.S. Department of Interior. U.S. Geological Survey. *Glacial Reconnaissance of Sequoia National Park, California.* Prepared by Fritiof Fryxell from the notes of Francois E. Matthes and other sources. USGS Professional Paper 504-A. Washington, D.C.: U.S. Government Printing Office, 1965.

U.S. Department of Interior. U.S. Geological Survey. *An Intensive Study of the Water Resources of a Part of Owens Valley, California*, by Charles H. Lee. Washington, D.C.: U.S. Government Printing Office, 1912.

U.S. Department of the Interior. U.S. Geological Survey and California Division of Mines and Geology. *The Sierra Nevada Batholith: A Synthesis of Recent Work Across the Central Part.* USGS Professional Paper 4514-D. Washington, D.C.: U.S. Government Printing Office, 1963.

U.S. Department of the Interior. U.S. Geological Survey and California Division of Mines and Geology. *Structural Geology and Volcanism of the Owens Valley Region, California: A Geophysical Study*, by L. C. Pakiser, M. F. Kane, and W. H. Jackson. USGS Professional Paper 438. Washington, D.C.: U.S. Government Printing Office, 1964.

Van Gelder, Richard G. *Mammals of the National Parks.* Baltimore: Johns Hopkins University Press, 1982.

Voegelin, Charles F. *Tubatulabal Grammar.* University of California Publications in American Archaeology and Ethnology, vol. 34, bk. 2. Berkeley: University of California Press, 1935.

Voegelin, Erminie W. *Tubatulabal Ethnography.* University of California Publications in Anthropological Records, vol. 2, bk. 1. Berkeley: University of California Press, 1938.

Von Sadovsky, Otto J. "The Discovery of California: Breaking the Silence of the Siberia-to-America Migrators." In *The Californians* 2, no. 6 (November–December 1984): 9–20.

Von Werlhof, Jay C. *Aboriginal Trails of the Kaweah Basin.* Report to Regional Archaeologist, National Park Service. Pamphlet. Visalia, Calif.: College of the Sequoias, 1961.

———. *Archaeological Investigations at Hospital Rock.* Report for National Park Service, Sequoia National Park, Department of Archaeology. Visalia, Calif.: College of the Sequoias, 1960.

———. "What We Found at Hospital Rock." In *The Kaweah Magazine* 1, no. 3 (September 1960): 17–22.

Walker, Ardis Manly. *Francisco Garces: A Pioneer Padre of Los Tulares.* Bakersfield, Calif.: Kern County Historical Society and the County of Kern, 1946.

Watkins, Francis E. "Indian Potters and Basket Makers of Southern California." In *California History Nugget* 7, no. 5 (February 1940): 151–57.

———. "Indians at Play." In *California History Nugget* 7, no. 6 (March 1940): 187–93.

Wernicke, Brian, et al. "Origin of High Mountains in the Continents: The Southern Sierra Nevada." In *Science* 271 (January 12, 1996): 190–93.

West, Kim. *Extinctions: Cycles of Life and Death Through Time* (1996). http://hoopermuseum.earthsci.carleton.ca//extinction/homepg.html

West, Tina. "The Life in the Basket." In *Sierra Heritage*, September–October 1997: 24–27.

Whitney, Stephen. *Sierra Club Naturalists' Guide to the Sierra Nevada*. San Francisco: Sierra Club Books, 1979.

Wilke, Philip J., and Harry W. Laughton. *The Expedition of Capt. J. W. Davidson from Fort Tejon to the Owens Valley in 1859*. Socorro, N.Mex.: Ballena Press, 1976.

Williams, Virginia. "Washtubs or Bathtubs? Ancient Basins Cause Scientific Debate." In *Fresno Bee*, August 9, 1970.

Willoughby, Nona C. "Division of Labor Among the Indians of California." In *California Indians*, vol 2. New York: Garland Publishers, 1974.

Wuerthner, George. *California's Sierra Nevada*. Helena, Mont.: American and World Geographic Publishing, 1993.

Younkin, Elva, ed. *Coso Rock Art: A New Perspective*. Ridgecrest, Calif.: Maturango Press, 1998.

Unpublished Materials

Bard, James C., et. al. "Kennedy Meadows Cultural Resources Data Recovery Project." Typescript report prepared by Kobari Environmental Management Corp., Hayward, Calif., for U.S. Department of Agriculture, Sequoia National Forest, 1985. Sequoia National Forest archives, Porterville, Calif.

Bates, Craig D. "A Historical View of Southern Sierra Miwok Dance and Ceremony." Manuscript, n.d. Yosemite National Park archives, Yosemite, Calif.

Berryman, Lorin E., and Albert B. Elsasser. "Terminus Dam Reservoir." Report prepared by the U.S. Army Corps of Engineers in cooperation with the National Park Service, n.d. Sequoia National Park archives, Three Rivers, Calif.

Bettinger, Robert L. "The Surface Archaeology of Owens Valley, Eastern California: Prehistoric Man-Land Relationships in the Great Basin." PhD diss., University of California, Riverside, 1975. Inyo National Forest archives, Bishop, Calif.

Burge, Thomas L., and William Mathews. "High Sierra Surveys in Kings Canyon National Park, 1997, 1998, and 1999." Paper presented at the 27th Great Basin Anthropological Conference, Ogden, Utah, October 2000.

Campbell, Charles W. "Origins and Ethnography of Prehistoric Man in the Owens Valley." Unpublished manuscript. Eastern California Museum, Independence, Calif., 1974.

Fenega, Franklin. "A Preliminary Account of the Archaeological Field Work Conducted in the Terminus Reservoir in Tulare County, California, in June and July 1950." Report for the Bureau of Land Management, 1950. BLM archives, Bakersfield, Calif.

Garfinkle, Alan P., Robert A. Schiffman, and Kelly R. McGuire. "Archaeological Investigations in the Southern Sierra Nevada: The Lamont Meadow and Morris Peak Segments of the Pacific Crest Trail." Report for the Bureau of Land Management, 1980. BLM archives, Bakersfield, Calif.

Goldberg, Susan K. "Cultural Resources Investigations for Proposed Amendment to the Haas-Kings River Project Application (FERC 1988) and the Balch Project License (FERC 175) II, Culture Site Records." Commissioned report by Infotec Research, Sonora, Calif., for Pacific Gas & Electric Company, 1986. Pacific Gas & Electric Company archives, San Francisco, Calif.

Halliday, William R. "Caves of California." Special report of the Western Speleological Survey for the National Speleological Society, 1962. Sequoia National Park archives, Three Rivers, Calif.

Jennings, Calvin H. "Archaeological Reconnaissance in the Camp Potwisha Vicinity, Sequoia National Park, California." Paper presented to Department of Anthropology, Colorado State University, 1973. Sequoia National Park Archives, Three Rivers, Calif.

————, and Patricia Kisling. "Archaeological Resources of the Mineral King District." Archaeology paper no. 29. California Archaeology Society, January 1971. U.S. Department of Agriculture archives, Washington, D.C.

Kipps, Jo Anne. "The Dinkey Creek Prehistoric Testing Program." Report prepared for Kings River Conservation District, Fresno, Calif., 1982. Sierra National Forest archives, Clovis, Calif.

McGuire, Kelly R., and Alan P. Garfinkle. "Archaeological Investigations in the Southern Sierra Nevada: The Bear Mountain Segment of the Pacific Crest Trail." Commissioned report for Bureau of Land Management, submitted 1980. BLM archives, Bakersfield, Calif.

————. "Archaeological Investigations in the Southern Sierra Nevada: The Kennedy Meadows/Rockhouse Basin Segment of the Pacific Crest Trail." Commissioned report for U.S. Department of Agriculture, Sequoia National Forest, submitted 1981. Sequoia National Forest archives, Porterville, Calif.

Merriam, C. Hart, and Zenaida Merriam Talbot. "Boundary Descriptions of California Indian Stocks and Tribes." Paper presented to Archaeological Research Facility, University of California–Berkeley, Department of Anthropology, 1974. Phoebe A. Hearst Museum of Anthropology archives, University of California–Berkeley.

Michaels, William. "At the Plow and in the Harvest Field: Indian Conflict and Accommodation in the Owens Valley 1860–1880." Master's thesis, University of Oklahoma, 1993.

Moratto, Michael J. 1972. "A Study of Prehistory in the Southern Sierra Nevada Foothills, California". PhD. diss., University of Oregon, 1972.

Palmer, John J. "Karst Resources: Their Management and Development in Sequoia and Kings Canyon National Parks." Paper prepared for Far West Regional Cave Management Symposium, October 23–27, 1979. Sequoia National Park archives, Three Rivers, Calif.

Peck, Billy J., et al. "Culture Resource Investigations for the North Fork Kern River, Tulare and Kern Counties, California." Commissioned report by Western Ecological Services for the U.S. Forest Service, Sequoia National Forest, February 1981. Archaeological and Environmental Services archives, Fresno, Calif.

Reynolds, Linda. "Heritage Resources Program Overview, Inyo National Forest, California and Nevada." Report for U.S. Department of Agriculture, Forest Service, Inyo National Forest, 1998. Inyo National Forest archives, Bishop, Calif.

Roper, C. Kristina, and David M. Graber. "Competition and Niche Overlap between Native Americans and Grizzly Bears on the Western Slope of the Sierra Nevada." Undated manuscript. Sequoia National Park archives, Three Rivers, Calif.

Stevens, Nathan. "Prehistoric Use of the Alpine Sierra Nevada." Master's thesis, California State University–Sacramento, 2002.

Stewart, Richard. "The Owens Valley Paiute." Unpublished oral history. Eastern California Museum, Independence, Calif., 1994.

Strong, Douglas Hillman. "A History of Sequoia National Park." Abstract of PhD diss., Syracuse University, 1964. Sequoia National Park archives, Three Rivers, Calif.

Theodoratus, Dorothea J., et al. "Cultural Resources Overview of the Southern Sierra Nevada: An Ethnographic, Archaeological, and Historical Study of the Sierra National Forest, Sequoia National Forest, and Bakersfield District of the Bureau of Land Management." Commissioned report by Theodoratus Cultural Research and Archaeological Consulting and Research Services for the U.S. Department of Agriculture, Forest Service, Bishop, Calif., 1984. Inyo National Forest archives, Bishop Calif.

———. "An Ethnohistoric Survey of the Dinkey Creek Hydroelectric Project." Commissioned report by Theodoratus Cultural Research and Archaeological Consulting and Research Services for Kings River Conservation District, Fresno, Calif., 1982. Sierra National Forest archives, Clovis, Calif.

———. "Ethnographic Cultural Resources Investigation of the Big Creek-Springville-Magunden and Big Creek-Rector-Vestal-Magunden Transmission Corridors." Commissioned report by Theodoratus Cultural Research for Southern California Edison Co., Rosemead, Calif., 1982. Sierra National Forest archives, Clovis, Calif.

Varner, Dudley M., and David R. Stuart. "A Survey of Archaeological and Historical Resources in the Central Yokohl Valley, Tulare County." Report for Laboratory of Archaeology, Department of Anthropology, California State University, Fresno, Calif., March 1975. Fresno State University Dept. of Anthropology archives.

Waterman, T. T. "Tubatulabal Texts, Vocabulary and Ethnographic Notes." Manuscript. Ca. 1915–16. Ethnological documents, University Archives. Bancroft Library, University of California–Berkeley.

Winter, Joseph Charles. "Aboriginal Agriculture in the Southwest and Great Basin." PhD diss., University of Utah, 1974.

Woolfenden, Wallace B. "The Role of Social Organization in Trans-Sierran Exchange Systems." Unpublished paper, n.d. Inyo National Forest archives, Bishop, Calif.

"Yosemite Nature Notes." Yosemite National Park newsletters, 1923–26. Yosemite National Park archives, Yosemite, Calif.

Index

About the Author

Louise A. Jackson's ties to the High Sierra region run deep; one ancestor homesteaded in the Kings River watershed and another in the Tule River watershed. Her childhood home stood at the base of the southern High Sierra. After receiving a B.A. in English and History at UCLA, Jackson spent most of her adult life exploring, researching, and writing about the Sierra Nevada. She currently resides in a 100-year-old adobe home in the foothill community of Three Rivers, California. Her published books include *Mineral King: the Story of Beulah* and *The Mule Men: A History of Stock Packing in the Sierra Nevada.*

CPSIA information can be obtained
at www.ICGtesting.com
Printed in the USA
FSHW022230050321
79195FS